From Ships to Sheep

The Story of Smallhythe

From Ships to Sheep

The Story of Smallhythe

by
Tony Buttler, Maurice Dalton, Susannah Mayor and Fred Walker

Conceived and compiled
by Maurice Dalton

Published with the support of

Commemorating the Great Fire and Rebuilding of
Smallhythe500
1514 -1515

First published in 2015
Reprinted in 2022

ISBN 978-0-9927656-9-9

Typeset in Baskerville Old Face 11pt

Designed by
Afterhours Artwork, Cranbrook, Kent
Email: *art@afterhours.myzen.co.uk*

Printed by
Printed Word Publishing, Hastings, East Sussex
www.printedwordpublishing.com

YouByYou Books, Biddenden, Kent
www.youbyyou.co.uk

Front Cover – Photograph © Fred Walker
Back Cover – Photograph © Laetitia Barnes

Contents

Contributors

Tony Buttler

Tony is an actuary who spent most of his working life as a consultant in the pension and financial services industries. He is a churchwarden of St. John the Baptist, Smallhythe, and the treasurer of a variety of local organisations including Tenterden and District National Trust Association and Tenterden and District Local History Society. Tony was also Treasurer of Smallhythe500.

Maurice Dalton LVO OBE

Maurice is a consultant on diplomatic, state and international protocol and has been resident close to Smallhythe since retiring from a career in HM Diplomatic Service. He is past chairman of Tenterden and District National Trust Association, a volunteer at Smallhythe Place (NT), where he is mostly engaged in historical research, and a life member of Tenterden and District Museum Association. He was chairman of Smallhythe500 during its two-year existence.

Susannah Mayor

Susannah is the House Steward at Smallhythe Place. She has worked for the National Trust for nearly 20 years in various capacities, most recently in conservation and care of collections. Susannah has a background in professional theatre and acting remains a major focus in her life. This, coupled with an interest in history, makes Smallhythe the perfect place for her to live and work. Susannah was a member of the committee of Smallhythe500.

Fred Walker

Fred served a shipbuilding apprenticeship on the Clyde whilst studying at the University of Glasgow. After graduating, he worked in a number of shipyards including Aberdeen where he was Shipyard Manager. In 1977 he became Consulting Naval Architect to the National Maritime Museum, Greenwich, and oversaw the building of a replica of the 1764 bark *Endeavour* in Western Australia, which has since circumnavigated the world. He restored old ships, designed historic replicas for many countries and was working on a range of projects at the time of his unexpected death in November 2020.

Smallhythe500

Smallhythe500 was a small not-for-profit group of local people formed for the specific purpose of commemorating in 2014-2015 the 500th anniversary of the destruction by fire of the very important medieval port and shipbuilding community of Smallhythe, the subsequent restoration of the village and its shipbuilding facilities and the building of the present church to replace the chapel lost in the fire.

Towards the end of 2013 representatives of the Parochial Church Council, Smallhythe Place (National Trust) and other interested people, looked at the possibilities for commemorating the fire and the rebuilding of the village and agreed that these momentous events in our local history should not go unmarked. They therefore established a small task force to work up a programme of events in 2014 and 2015 to commemorate or otherwise mark the quincentenary of the Great Fire and the residents' response to it. The task force was chaired by Maurice Dalton and two other contributors to this book – Tony Buttler and Susannah Mayor – were members of the group.

Their first action was to try to bring the story of Smallhythe to as many local people as possible in the shortest period of time. Working closely with the curator of Tenterden and District Museum, the Media Centre and various staff members and pupils of Homewood School and Sixth Form Centre, Tenterden, as well as with Smallhythe Church and Smallhythe Place, they produced new information panels for the Museum, Church and Smallhythe Place covering, inter alia, the history of Smallhythe, the Great Fire and rebuilding of Smallhythe, the history of Smallhythe Church, shipbuilding at Smallhythe, the Cinque Ports and story of Smallhythe Place. Homewood School in Tenterden designed and printed the information display panels for Tenterden Museum and Smallhythe Church, designed the extra large display panels for Smallhythe Place and made the special framework on which the panels are displayed at Smallhythe Place.

Smallhythe500 arranged two permanent reminders of the importance of Smallhythe in the Plantagenet and Tudor period, as the group's legacy to the village and people of Smallhythe. On 31 July 2015, the 500th anniversary of the Great Fire of Smallhythe, the Mayor of Tenterden, Councillor Pamela Smith, and the Chairman of Smallhythe500, Maurice Dalton, unveiled a jointly funded commemorative plaque installed on the bridge at Smallhythe. Later in 2015, Smallhythe500 funded the publication of this book, the production of which had been conceived and co-ordinated by Maurice Dalton.

To conclude the programme of events, in October 2015 Smallhythe500 staged a unique concert in Smallhythe Church during which key elements of the history of Smallhythe were presented by Ian Klemen, a well-known local actor, interspersed with choral music of the times performed by Tenterden Singers.

All of this would not have been possible without the financial support of the Canterbury Diocese Mission Resources Fund, Kent County Council (through Councillor Mike Hill) and Ashford Borough Council (through councillors Mike Bennett and Jill Hutchinson) and donations from individuals in the Tenterden area, including a very generous contribution from Sir Michael Uren.

The members of the Smallhythe500 task force hope that the programme of commemorative events held in 2014 and 2015 and the publication of this book will ensure that the story of Smallhythe's first millennium, not least the national importance of the shipbuilders of Smallhythe in the Plantagenet and Tudor period, will never be forgotten.

Timeline

English and *Scottish* Monarchs			
Alfred the Great (871-899)	9th C		First English monarch to deploy ships against a foreign foe
	10th C		Possible origin of "Ships' Service" to provide English monarchs with naval power
	11th C		
Edward the Confessor (1014-1066)			Origin of Cinque Ports Confederation
	12th C		
Henry II (1154-1189)		1155	English naval force raised
	13th C		
		1212	First English naval base, at Portsmouth
		1287	"Great Storm" hits Cinque Ports
	14th C		
		1332	Knelle Dam constructed
Henry IV (1399-1413)	15th C		
James 1 (1406-1437)			Scottish Navy founded under James I and developed under his successors
		1410	*Marie*, first Royal Ship built at Smallhythe for an English Monarch
Henry V (1413-1422)			
		c1415	William Caxton born, in Tenterden?
		1416	Royal Ships *Jesus* and *The George* built at Smallhythe
Henry VI (1422-1461)			
James II (1437-1460)		1449	Tenterden (including Smallhythe) becomes a member of the Cinque Ports
James III (1460-1488)			
Edward IV (1461-1470)			
Henry VI (1470-1471)			
Edward IV (1471-1483)			
Edward V (1483-1483)			
Richard III (1483 -1485)			
Henry VII (1485-1509)		1496	First English dry dock, at Portsmouth
James IV (1488-1513)			
	16th C		Emergence of permanent English Navy from five centuries of "Ships' Service"
Henry VIII (1509-1547)			
		1511	Launch in Scotland of *Great Michael* then the largest ship in Europe

Monarch	Century	Year	Event
James V (1513-1542)		1514	Launch in Woolwich of *Henri Grace a Dieu*, then the largest warship in the world
		1515	Smallhythe destroyed by fire on 31 July and subsequently rebuilt
		1516-7	Construction begins of present church at Smallhythe
		1515-20	Probable construction of Smallhythe Place and Priest's House
Mary, Queen of Scots (1542-1567)		1545	Royal Ship *Grand Mistress* built at Smallhythe
		1546	Royal Ship *Great Gallyon* built at Smallhythe (the last)
Edward VI (1547-1553)			
Mary I (1553-1558)			
Elizabeth I (1558-1603)		1596	Last deployment of Smallhythe "Ship Service" vessels, in raid on Cadiz
James VI (1567-1625)	17th C		
		1603	Union of crowns of England and Scotland
James I (1603-1625)			
Charles I (1625-1649)		1635	Knelle Dam breached
Council of State (1649-1653)			
Oliver Cromwell, Lord Protector (1653-1658)			
Richard Cromwell, Lord Protector (1658-1659)			
Council of State (1659-1660)			
Charles II (1660-1685)		1660	English Navy becomes (English) Royal Navy
James II (1685-1688)			
William III and Mary II (1689-1702)	18th C		
Anne (1702-1714)			
		1707	Union of England and Scotland Formation of Royal Navy by merger of Royal Scots Navy and the (English) Royal Navy
	19th C		
Victoria (1837-1901)		1899	Purchase by Ellen Terry of Smallhythe Place and, subsequently, Priest's House and Yew Tree Cottage at Smallhythe
Edward VII (1901-1910)	20th C		
George V (1910-1936)		1928	Death of Ellen Terry at Smallhythe Place
		1929	Smallhythe Place opened as Ellen Terry memorial museum and Barn Theatre established in the grounds
Edward VIII (1936-1936)			
George VI (1936-1952)		1939	National Trust accepts Smallhythe Place, Priest's House and other properties
Elizabeth II (1952-)			
	21st C	2001	Chapel Down Winery established in Smallhythe

Introduction

It is hard to imagine now, but at the beginning of the 16th century Smallhythe in the south of Kent was a thriving port and a major centre of shipbuilding. Located on the north bank of the River Rother, it was the port for the town of Tenterden, three miles to the north and, more widely, for the area known as the Weald of Kent. Two hundred years earlier, in the 14th century, the wool trade had brought riches to Tenterden, and the village of Smallhythe grew on the trade that passed through its port.

In medieval times, the River Rother traced a broad winding swathe across the marshlands that dominated this part of Kent and sea-going vessels could easily reach as far upriver as Smallhythe. The community's location on firm ground at the edge of the marshlands made it an ideal place for vessels engaged in trade around the coast or across the English Channel to load and unload their goods in safety. Indeed, part of the village's name "hythe" is derived from the word for "haven".

Smallhythe was not just a convenient and natural place for a port. Since the beginning of the 15th century it had also been a place for the building and repairing of ships and over the next century became one of the most important shipbuilding centres in England. At its height Smallhythe was probably the third most important

builder of ships for English monarchs from Henry IV to Henry VIII, ranking behind Deptford and Woolwich.

However, on 31 July 1515, during the reign of Henry VIII, the village and shipbuilding facilities of Smallhythe were destroyed by fire. Remarkably, the villagers resolved to rebuild everything – and they did just that.

Smallhythe is very different today. Much of the land to the south of Smallhythe has been drained and reclaimed for agriculture and vessels are now unable to navigate the waterways – mostly drainage channels – that lie between the village and the English Channel. There is now no obvious sign of the medieval port and shipbuilding facilities and, consequently, outside the local area their existence is almost totally unknown. However, we hope that the commemorative plaque installed in July 2015 on the present-day bridge over the last remnant of the River Rother at Smallhythe will be a lasting reminder of times past.

One of the challenges encountered in preparing this book was the name of our village. Two forms are in use today: "Small Hythe" and "Smallhythe". Both are to be seen on maps, road signs and street names. In the past, the name has appeared in many other forms and a note of these, together with some other possible variants, was compiled by Archaeology South East (University College London) for their 2005 report on Smallhythe. A selection of them is reproduced here and on the cover of this book. Faced with so many variants, it was thought that it might be appropriate to use the form that was in use when Smallhythe was at its peak in the Middle Ages but it was quickly found that there was no consistency of spelling at that time. As was so often the case, the spelling varied from writer to writer and often depended on how the scribe heard the word(s) or on how well an individual had mastered the intricacies of English spelling. The next idea was to follow the lead of the Ordnance Survey and use whatever form was shown on their modern maps. This did not help – both forms of the word are used on OS maps.

Our final thought was to use the form that present day residents use. The vast majority of those canvassed used "Smallhythe" and it is this form that has been used throughout this book.

The purpose of this book, made possible by the financial support of Smallhythe500, is to inform, entertain and, hopefully, to be a lasting reminder of the role played by Smallhythe over the last thousand years, particularly during the Middle Ages, not only in the economy of south Kent and the Weald but also in the defence of the Realm.

When the writers set out to prepare this book they soon became aware that there were very few extant records of events in Smallhythe during the period when the village was an important port and centre of shipbuilding. Those records that did exist were mostly confined to notes and entries in the records of other communities in the area. Any Smallhythe records that may have existed are presumed to have been lost in the fire that swept through the local archives in the Court Hall in Tenterden in 1660. The writers have therefore not been able to undertake much new research but, having drawn on material already in the public domain, they have, in some cases, reached new conclusions.

This book is not and was never intended to be a complete and comprehensive study of the life and times of Smallhythe. Its genesis lies in the material that the contributors assembled in connection with a number of projects and events

surrounding the 500th anniversary of the Great Fire of Smallhythe. The book looks at the major elements in Smallhythe's history as well as the influence of Tenterden and the Confederation of the Cinque Ports on Smallhythe but does not profess to cover all and every aspect thereof. The lack of primary evidence makes a deep and authoritative assessment something of a challenge but those seeking more information on Smallhythe would be well advised to turn to the report produced by Archaeology South East for the National Trust in 2005 and step off from there.

It is hoped that everyone will find this book a readable and enjoyable ramble through Smallhythe's remarkable contribution to our local and national history. Indeed, it might inspire others to continue the search for hard facts to fill the many gaps in our current knowledge. Smallhythe is an unlikely place to have had such a nationally important past but with the publication of this book it is hoped that its story will remain alive for many generations to come.

A tranquil scene from the rustic past

CHAPTER 1

A Remarkable Journey Through Time

Maurice Dalton

Smallhythe is a small village or hamlet, hidden away on a small peninsular of firm land, three miles south of the town of Tenterden in Kent. The peninsular links the northwest fringe of the marshy area known generally as Romney Marsh with the uplands of the Weald of Kent.

The surprises start with its age. Smallhythe is known to have been in existence by the mid-13th century. It was an important ferry crossing point to the Isle of Oxney to the south, and an equally important port for goods and materials being transported to and from Tenterden and the Weald.

For much of the second half of the Middle Ages, Smallhythe benefitted from being on the north bank of a broad and deep river, the River Rother. The natural course of the Rother was to the south of the Isle of Oxney but between 1332, when the Knelle Dam was built across the river, and 1635, when the dam was deliberately breached, the river flowed to the north of Oxney, sweeping past Smallhythe, Reading Street, Ebony, Stone and Appledore on its way to the sea near Rye. It was during this 300-year period that Smallhythe harboured another surprise – it was a busy local port and a builder of ships, including warships for some of the Plantagenet and Tudor monarchs, two surprising historical roles which are now almost forgotten outside the local area.

Today the river valley at Smallhythe is occupied by sheep, rather than ships, grazing on reclaimed land that is drained by the Reading Sewer (sewer is the local word for a drainage canal) and its tributaries. The slopes to the north, resting on underlying Wadhurst Clay, are used for a mixture of pasture, woodland, arable farming and vineyards producing some of the finest English wine. It is hard to imagine that where there are now fields of sheep there was once a wide tidal channel with ships coming and going. Occasionally, however, flooding of the flat fields between Smallhythe and the Isle of Oxney gives the present day observer an inkling of the watery scene that would have greeted a visitor 500 years ago.

Smallhythe floods in 1925

The coastline of south-east England today contrasted with the heavily indented coast of the 13th century

The Marshes

O ver the last 2,000 years, there have been many changes in the marshlands between Hythe in Kent and Rye in East Sussex, some occurring naturally and others as the result of human intervention.

In the mid-13th century a number of storms caused the sea to break through the coastal shingle banks, flooding significant areas of land and turning it into marsh. The Great Storm of 1287 left New Romney flooded and the harbour was filled with silt, sand, mud and debris. Old Winchesea was also flooded and the course of the River Rother changed to enter the sea near Rye instead of at New Romney. However, despite their destructive power, the storms also helped to build up protective shingle banks along the coastline that was then developing.

By the 14th century, several of the marshes had been reclaimed by "innings", a process of building embankments around a marsh and draining the land by a system of dykes and one-way sluices or drains in the sea wall. This process continued over the following centuries as did the deposition of shingle along the coastline and today the marshland, generally known as the Romney Marsh but actually comprising several marshes, is protected from sea incursions and flooding by sea walls and a network of rivers and drainage channels and ditches.

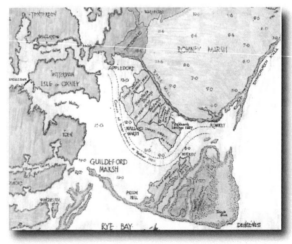

The course of the River Rother through the marshes

Shipbuilding

H ugh Roberts, in his publication *Tenterden – the First Thousand Years* notes that maritime activity existed at Smallhythe from 1326. The safe harbour, nearby oak forests and the sloping shore needed for slipways provided all that was necessary for shipbuilding. The first mention of vessels built at Smallhythe was in 1342, shortly after the building of the Knelle Dam. The earliest record of a named ship being

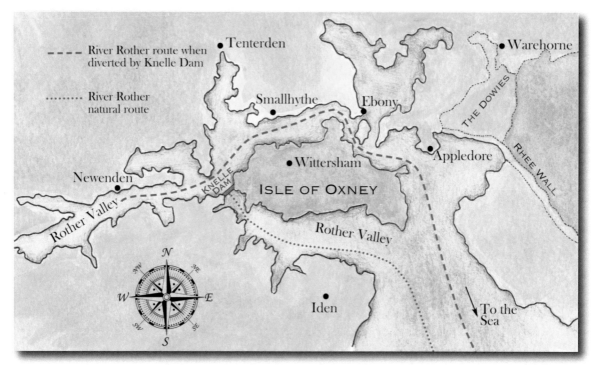

The Knelle Dam and courses of the River Rother

built at Smallhythe is in the New Romney town accounts which record expenditure on a barge, the *Eneswythe* built at Smallhythe in 1400. There are no known records of the depth of the river but at Smallhythe it is likely to have been about 6.5 metres at high water and 2 metres at low water, sufficient for the largest ships of Medieval England to be built or repaired at Smallhythe. Whatever the actual depth, in the 14th and 15th centuries the Rother was wide enough and deep enough for the largest ships of medieval England to be built and launched at Smallhythe.

The nearest town to Smallhythe was, and still is, Tenterden, a town made rich by its role in the wool trade. In May 1337 King Edward III issued an edict to encourage Flemish cloth workers to come to England and Kent was selected as the centre for broadcloth manufacture. The Weald of Kent acquired the reputation for making strong, durable, broadcloth of good mixture and colours. The export of wool from Tenterden was channelled through the port at Smallhythe, as were exports of timber and charcoal. By the middle of the 14th century,

Smallhythe's role as Tenterden's port was of considerable importance and by 1381, the year of the Peasants' Revolt, Smallhythe was perceived as a municipal centre in its own right. The port was handling considerable shipborne commerce.

Tenterden and the Peasants' Revolt of 1381

The revolt, which spread across much of the country, had various causes, including the socio-economic and political tensions generated by the Black Death in the 1340s, the high taxes resulting from the conflict with France during the Hundred Years War, and instability within the leadership of London. Locally, much of Tenterden's wool-trade wealth was enjoyed by a privileged few. The ordinary townsfolk's resentment of their position led to some of them joining the 1381 Peasants' Revolt, in which Wat Tyler marched a group of protesters on Canterbury and then London to oppose the institution of a poll tax.

Foreign immigrants, particularly from the Low Countries, took up residence there in order to do business.

From the beginning of the 15th century, the settlement was substantial enough to be called a town yet it never escaped from playing a subservient role in its relationship with Tenterden. When Tenterden became a member of the Cinque Ports confederation in 1449, Smallhythe underpinned the dominant partner's ability to meet its obligations. [See Chapter 3, Smallhythe and The Cinque Ports.]

The shipbuilding area at Smallhythe

Between the 14th and 16th centuries Smallhythe was a thriving community of around 200 people. Most of the permanent residents would have been involved in shipbuilding and the port. By or in the 15th century, local society at Smallhythe was dominated by several families with shipbuilding interests. There was probably also a transient population of workers when large ships were built. The community built its own chapel and financed its own chaplain, rather than attending the parish church at Tenterden. In the mid-1500s an inquiry concerning the chapel at Smallhythe noted there were 60 to 100 "houseling people" in Smallhythe, that is 60 to 100 communicants. The main settlement was centred along the road leading down to the River Rother and along *Strand Syde*, a road running along its northern bank. It must have been a lively and noisy place. Alas, everything came to an abrupt stop on 31 July 1515, when much of Smallhythe was destroyed by fire, including the

shipbuilding facilities and the chapel. The fire was doubtless a disaster of enormous impact but, fortunately, the community had grown rich on the shipbuilding industry and, as we shall see in Chapter 4, was well placed immediately to set about replacing what had been lost.

The Chapel

We do not know which homes, buildings, shipbuilding facilities were actually lost in the fire, except for the Chapel at Smallhythe. Church records show that, although the Chapel building lost in the fire was over one hundred years old, it was not until 1506 that it had been formally licensed to hold divine services. Having only recently won this right, after the fire the people of Smallhythe immediately set out to build a bigger and better replacement for its predecessor. No doubt part of the reason for their enthusiasm was that they wished to ensure that the absence of a place of worship did not cause them to lose the right to appoint their own chaplain, a right unique in the whole county.

The building they constructed, a brick-built Chapel dedicated to St John the Baptist, still stands today, a testimony to the people of Smallhythe who decided to build for longevity and, in particular, to use brick as the main structural material. The unusual stepped gable ends to the roof are thought to be the work of – or to have been influenced by – Dutch immigrants living in the area. How much they were involved is not known but they must have had very good standing in the community to be permitted to incorporate such a clear reference to their homeland in the design of the new chapel. You will find further details in Chapter 5.

The Decline of Smallhythe

The decline of Smallhythe as a prosperous centre of shipbuilding and busy port started in the 16th century when the river began to silt up. The causes were both natural and manmade. Among the latter was the practice of ships' crews throwing ballast into the river. The silt increasingly restricted navigation and limited the size of vessels that could be floated at Smallhythe.

Nonetheless, significant ships continued to be constructed on the river bank and Henry VIII commissioned further, smaller vessels at Smallhythe including the 450-ton *Grand Mistress* in 1545 and the 300-ton *Great Gallyon* in 1546. The latter was still a sizeable vessel and was capable of carrying 140 men. Further information about shipbuilding at Smallhythe is in Chapter 2.

Despite the impact of silting on shipbuilding, Smallhythe continued to operate as a port and builder of smaller craft until the 1630s, when with the deliberate breaching of the Knelle Dam in 1635 the River Rother reverted to its original course south of the Isle of Oxney. The consequential loss of water at Smallhythe hastened its decline as a port, shipbuilding centre and community. A similar fate befell Reading Street and Appledore, a short distance downstream from Smallhythe.

There is much uncertainty about the population and infrastructure of Smallhythe at this time. Local records lodged in the Court Hall in Tenterden were lost when prisoners held in the room above the Hall set fire to the building on 19 March 1661.

However, with the continuing reclamation of the marshes, Smallhythe's interests would have turned towards agriculture, focussing on reclamation along the former course of the River Rother and the use of the reclaimed land for grazing. The population shrank and the community became mainly one of farm workers and shepherds, with ownership of the land dominated by lessees and graziers from Tenterden. Some small-scale shipbuilding continued at Smallhythe into the 20th century but was confined to small boats and river barges for local use, the design of which had remained almost unchanged.

The ferry to the Isle of Oxney continued to operate until at least the mid-17th century but a 1688 map shows that it had, by then, been replaced by a bridge. The toll was transferred from the ferry to the bridge and remained until 1932.

Barges continued to sail from Rye to Smallhythe, via the network of drainage channels up to 1924. Typical of such craft were the two sailing barges owned and operated by Mr W S Body and his sons at the beginning of the 20th century. The photograph below shows one of their barges at Smallhythe in December 1905, manoeuvring under the gaze of Mr Body himself, on the right bank. Their barges normally plied between Potman's Heath Wharf and Rolvenden carrying coal and building materials upstream and corn downstream.

The photograph is helpfully annotated by Ellen Terry, the great Victorian actress who owned the house in the background between 1899 and 1928, and gives us the exact month and

Mr W S Body's Barge at Smallhythe Bridge, December 1905

Ships' nails found at Smallhythe in 2015

year in which this vessel sailed to Smallhythe. The small building behind the man at the tiller of the barge is the toll-keeper's house. In their own ways, both the barge and the house represent the last vestiges of the remarkable contribution that Smallhythe made to local and national interests over a period of many centuries.

Smallhythe, like several other ports in the South East, has experienced great changes in its fortunes, livelihood and population over the years. Various influences, including river silt, the establishment of a standing navy and competition with other better-placed ports each had a role to play in transforming a safe haven, thriving port and builder of ships for the Crown into a quiet agricultural community of about 50 households spread thinly across a gently undulating hillside some seven miles inland from the English Channel.

All trace of the port has gone and only a few ships' nails and faint depressions in the ground indicate where shipbuilding took place. Where once there was a broad river, navigable all the way to the sea, there are now only drainage channels. Looking at the calm and quiet countryside today, it really is difficult to imagine the bustle and noise of the port and shipbuilding activities of 500 years ago. Nonetheless, the small community is justifiably proud of its history and the significant role that Smallhythe played in the Middle Ages both as a port and, most especially, as one of the country's leading builders of ships for the defence of Plantagenet and Tudor England.

Royal Ships of Smallhythe

During the 15th and 16th centuries a number of ships were commissioned from Smallhythe by the monarch of the day, including the 1,000 ton *Jesus* which, at the time, was the second biggest ship built in medieval England.

In the early 16th century Smallhythe craftsmen walked to Woolwich to assist with the building of a further Royal Ship, the *Henry Grace a Dieu* (1,400 tons), also known as the *Great Harry*, which, when completed in 1514, was the largest warship in Europe. Some of the timbers for the ship were prepared at Smallhythe and then sent to Woolwich by sea.

Smallhythe – From Ships to Sheep

During repair work at St Dunstan's Church, Snargate, a painting in terracotta colours of a
Great Ship was discovered on the north wall. It has been dated to around 1500 and is a good likeness
of one of the Great Ships built at Smallhythe (six miles west) in the same period

CHAPTER 2

The Medieval Shipyards of Smallhythe

Fred Walker

Smallhythe, now a tiny land-locked village on the edge of the Romney Marsh, has a remarkable history and can claim to have taken a leading part in the founding of the Royal Navy. While readers may be aware that there are long lost shipyards in the south-east corner of Kent, few realise that 500 years ago shipbuilding – on a near industrial scale – was practised at Smallhythe, a parish of Tenterden. Indeed, if one excludes the Royal Dockyards, Smallhythe was the largest English shipbuilding site in the early 16th century. It is known that three Kings – Henry V, Henry VII and Henry VIII – all placed work there.

Evidence that Smallhythe was a shipbuilding site

Despite the fruits of increasing geographical and historical research, our knowledge of the Smallhythe shipyards remains limited, and any analysis can be little more than a tentative foray into their probable layout and administration. Information has been culled from a wide range of sources and we are fairly certain as to the position of at least two construction sites and also of the means of building, launching and ultimately moving the "new-builds" from Smallhythe and nearby Reading Street down the River Rother to

the sea. A conjectural portrait has been developed of the 15th and 16th century shipyards which will have to be tested in the light of ever-improving historical and geomorphological information, and of our ever-increasing understanding of medieval shipbuilding practice.

The evidence for shipbuilding at Smallhythe is conclusive: County records mention a wide range of industries which cluster round the ship construction sites, including timber suppliers, animal haulage teams (the transport contractors of medieval times), charcoal burners, iron smelters, blacksmiths, rope and canvas makers, sail-makers and so on. Recent investigations have unearthed iron spikes and nails as used in shipbuilding in the Smallhythe area and, as an exercise, some of the roadways of 500 years ago have been walked over, checked and found suitable for the haulage of heavy lumber by horses and oxen.

The most compelling evidence of all is from records of the reigns of Henry VII and Henry VIII which confirm that ships of the fledgling English Navy were constructed in the area. The Anthony Roll indicates several ships constructed at Smallhythe, Reading Street and Winchelsea. It is possible that some of the Winchelsea hulls were in fact built and launched at Smallhythe and then towed unfinished to Winchelsea for outfitting (that is the completion of

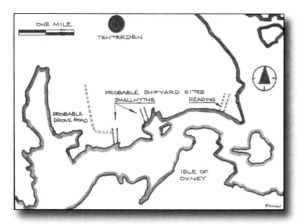

A conjectural plan of Smallhythe and Reading Street in the 15th and 16th centuries, showing likely positions of shipbuilding sites and the Drove Road north from Smallhythe

the internal work) and for masting and rigging. Such a situation would arise when lack of water at Smallhythe forced the builders to keep the ships as light as possible enabling them to sail downstream with the least possible draft.

Why Smallhythe was suitable for shipbuilding in medieval times

In medieval times, shipyards could be found in many parts of the coastline of Europe. Smallhythe, as with these other places, was subject to the following standard requirements:

Adequate Water – enabling ships to be launched safely, subsequently moored (preferably afloat) for the weeks or months while the finishing touches were bestowed on the new hull, and then with adequate water at high tide for the ship to leave for her appointed delivery voyage along the Rother Water and then southwards on the Appledore Water to Winchelsea and the sea.

Strong and Stable Land for the Construction Site – the ground which becomes compacted with regular use has to bear intense point loads from the ship under construction. It should have a gentle slope (known as the declivity) to the water's edge to ensure the completed hull could be launched with the minimum of effort.

Storage Space – as shipbuilding is a complex assembly process, adequate space is vital, not just for the myriad of small items required in construction, but also for the vast quantities of lumber arriving on a daily basis from the forests. Once cut and prepared this material, now known as dressed timber, had to be stacked carefully to dry out partially before being used on the ship.

Access – important for delivery of timber and other materials. In those days great reliance was placed on the Drove Roads – the "motorways" of the age, following routes with the easiest gradients for the ox and horse-drawn trailers in regular use.

Availability of Materials – was vital. Delays in supply – always unacceptable – were overcome by holding adequate stock and by regular deliveries of items as diverse as rope and tar, iron pigs and lumber. Timber came in two forms, long tree trunks for planks and pieces known as "grown timber" for the many small shaped items like knees, brackets, breasthooks and so on. The main timbers were:

Oak – a general purpose timber for keels, frames and shell planking and occasionally for decks.
Elm – a tough straight-grained timber for keels and parts of a ship subject to abrasion.
Fir – for masts and spars and sometimes decks and planking.

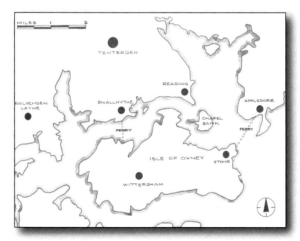

Possible extent of tidal waters around the Isle of Oxney 14th-15th centuries. Shorelines based on Ordnance Survey map 10-metre contour

Smallhythe – From Ships to Sheep

The Anthony Roll

Grand Mistress

Known also as Graunde Masterys, *this 450 ton galleasse was built in Smallhythe for King Henry VIII and is celebrated for all time by inclusion on the Anthony Roll of Henry VIII's Navy*

In 1546, a clerk in the Ordnance Office, rejoicing in the name of Anthony Anthony, produced a pictorial survey of 58 ships in the fleet of King Henry VIII. Each ship is shown in elevation with the starboard side in view, so the ships are pointing to the right hand side of the page; almost all are drawn with flags flying, an anchor line extended and a pinnace or jolly boat attached at the stern. Ranking as one of the earliest public relations exercises for the Navy, the Roll endeared Anthony to the King who had by then realised the importance of naval power.

One drawback of the Roll is that all the ships look alike, bringing into question the accuracy of the draughtsmanship. Any such problem is compensated for by the wealth of written detail regarding guns and equipment and by the listing of the complement carried, broken into 'soldiours, marrynars and gonnars'.

The drawings were on a single roll of vellum, which in the course of time was divided into three parts; the first and third now deposited in the Pepys Library of Magdalene College, Cambridge and the second or middle roll in the British Library, London.

Self-Sustaining – the community had to have inbuilt resources: A population large enough to maintain local services and supply labour and apprentices to the shipyards and housing to meet the needs of a thriving local community whilst accommodating influxes of itinerant labour in times of high production. In all respects Smallhythe came up to the mark.

How ships got to the sea

Standing in the garden of Smallhythe Place today and looking south over the low and fertile fields leading to the Isle of Oxney, one could be excused for doubting the existence of these medieval Kent shipyards, a doubt exacerbated by sight of the tiny stream at the bottom of the garden - the Reading Sewer, moving in a sluggish manner. The extreme flatness of the fields indicates they are polders, or land reclaimed from the sea, similar to the much larger areas found today in The Netherlands. This dramatic change has been the subject of considerable study over the past hundred years, and doubtless will continue to intrigue scientists for years to come.

The polder lands beyond Smallhythe with the former Isle of Oxney rising in the distance. In the foreground is the tiny Reading Sewer marking the original northern boundary of Smallhythe Water

The shipbuilding era of Smallhythe is assumed to have been from around the 1350s until just after the 1550s, and probably peaked in the 1400s. The number of ships constructed is unlikely to have been more than 250, many of which would have been local trading barges and small coastal fishing craft. Small vessels did not create much interest and few records exist.

For around 200 years the valley between Smallhythe and the Isle of Oxney was navigable, and ships leaving Smallhythe (or Reading) would sail eastwards and on passing Appledore turn south in what may have been called Appledore Water. This channel seems to have been in fairly continuous use during the shipbuilding years, and at high tide the depth of water would have been adequate for ships bringing cargoes to Appledore, Reading Street and Smallhythe or other minor ports, or for vessels being delivered from the shipyards and on occasion returning for repairs. The twice-daily ebb and flow of tides would have kept the channels clear of sand and silt, while any small shoals which might have developed from time to time would have been cleared by hand dredging.

The actual depth of the waterways is unknown, but is unlikely to have been more than a few metres at high tide, as shown in the diagram (opposite). Rather similar to Rye Harbour, at low water springs the Smallhythe Channel would have at most a couple of metres of water in the main channel, whilst at high water springs this would be several metres in depth. The difference is known as the 'range of tides' and at Smallhythe the maximum range at spring tides is likely to have been no more than four and a half metres – and at neap tides a mere two metres. These estimates are based on our understanding that the maximum tidal range at the nearest part of the English Channel would have been nearer seven metres.

Provided there were no barriers in the channel, ships with a draft of up to three and a half metres could have been moved from Smallhythe during the window of opportunity of about two hours either side of high water springs. While tidal heights can be predicted with some certainty, from time to time (and usually owing to weather conditions) they fail to reach expectation and ships might then have been grounded on the passage and have to wait for two weeks or even as long as a month until one of the following spring tides gave adequate water for open passage to the sea.

It is likely that shipbuilders would have kept the outfitting of their larger vessels to a minimum to ensure the displacement and also the draft was as small as possible. Some of the larger ships would not have armament placed aboard until delivered to Winchelsea and on occasions the masts and spars might not be shipped until the inland voyage was completed.

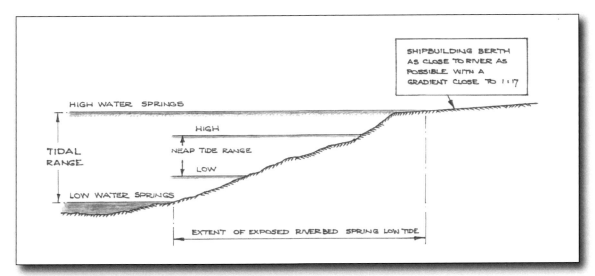

During the 15th and 16th centuries, the maximum tidal range off Winchelsea and Rye would have been around 6.5 metres, and indeed the range remains close to this today. Moving inland, the tidal range reduces owing to the resistance of curved channels and the sheer friction of moving masses of water. Subject to further investigations, it is likely that the maximum tidal range at Smallhythe would have been just over 4 metres. This would have enabled the largest warships to be moved, but only at high water spring tides

The ship movement would require oarsmen using long oars, known as sweeps, working on the new ship as well as small attendant boats and they would travel as swiftly as possible, and with great luck make Winchelsea in one tide. Otherwise the ship would be moored and might have to lie on the channel bed for some hours until the water returned.

There were no formal tidal predictions, and the shipwright in charge would have to work out suitable days for ship movements based on long experience of the river, coupled with knowledge of the cycles of the moon.

Two explanations exist for the closure of the navigable channel, the first is a breach occurring in the dam at Maytham Wall sometime after 1600 which changed the shape of the channel, while the other was the deliberate breach of Knelle Dam in 1635 in a vain attempt to reinstate the navigable waterway. Around this time the shape of the navigable portion of the Marshes changed dramatically with some parts becoming subject to flooding, whilst other parts drained. Smallhythe as a port diminished gradually and by the late 17th century, the ferry to the Isle of Oxney had been replaced by a bridge. The land profiles away from the channels will have altered

little over the years, and therefore higher ground would look much the same as today. Similarly (but subject to further research) the sea levels are unlikely to have altered during the shipbuilding period by any more than a centimetre or two.

The shipbuilding families

Formal records of the known 200 years of shipbuilding on the Rother are few and far between. We are struggling to identify less than twenty per cent of the ships built, and similarly are unable to name many of the residents of the community. Of the Master Shipwrights we know only two of the family names – Hoggskynes and Brygandyne.

Hugh Roberts in his book *Tenterden: The First Thousand Years*, relates that in June 1421, King Henry V on a visit to Smallhythe authorised a pension of 4d a day for John Hoggskynes, master carpenter, *"because in labouring long about the ships he is much shaken and worsten of body"*. Roberts suggests that this may have come through the monumental effort to complete Smallhythe's largest ship, the *Jesus* of 1,000 tons just five years earlier. King Henry VII is known to have visited Smallhythe in 1487, but according to Roberts, he made other visits to inspect the ships and is reputed to have had a friendly relationship with the shipbuilders.

The Brygandyne family was well known in Smallhythe with at least four related men who may all have served in the shipyards. The most prominent was Robert Brygandyne, a master shipwright in the 1480s and early 1490s, who in 1495 entered royal service as Henry VII's Clerk of the King's Ships, based at Portsmouth. This senior appointment enabled him to oversee many important tasks including supervising the construction of England's first dry-dock at Portsmouth in 1496. At that time he was responsible for the building of the great ship *Henri Grace a Dieu* at Woolwich on the Thames: the *Great Harry,* as she was nicknamed, had her timbers cut in Smallhythe and transported by sea to Woolwich and further subcontracting included the refurbishment of old anchors for the ship by the blacksmiths in Smallhythe. In 1512 a large draft of shipwrights was assembled in the Tenterden area before they walked to Woolwich to work on the great ship; clearly Robert Brygandyne favoured the men of Smallhythe and used his considerable authority to ensure work came their way. Robert Brygandyne remained in his post until 1523 having served Henry VII and Henry VIII.

Royal patronage continued and when Henry VIII came to Smallhythe on 28 August 1537, he was received by John Brygandyne, one of the following generation of Master Shipwrights. But by then the glory days were almost at an end.

The Master Shipwright

Always the key man in any shipyard, medieval or otherwise, the Master Shipwright had to ensure all work was carried out to the highest standard and that ships were delivered on time and at an agreed cost. Along with the privilege of absolute control of the shipyard, he had the ultimate responsibility of striving to make the business efficient and ensuring it played a worthwhile role in the relatively small community in which his family and friends made their livelihood.

The Master Shipwright was responsible for the selection of trees to be felled, a task that was critical to the success of the shipyard. Such work would take him on long and tough hikes through the forests of the South East to identify long trunks free of knots and timbers with unusual shapes (known as grown timber) that could be used for knees or brackets. His main tasks were the oversight of the shipyard, negotiations with contractors and to ensure there was suitable credit (hopefully in coin) to maintain steady employment. As one who had risen through the ranks, the Master Shipwright would know how to handle the normal problems of petty pilferage, insubordination, absenteeism, incompetence and drunkenness. However in the 15th and 16th centuries he was a powerful employer as there were few restraints regarding punishment and dismissal and, in a fragile local economy, unemployment was a serious matter.

The saw pit and two men on the double-ended saw

It was usual for the Master Shipwright to lease the ground on which the ship was to be built, such as at Smallhythe around 1497 when the keel of the *Mary Fortune* was laid. The Master Shipwright was one of the Brygandyne family and he rented the land from another member of the same family. Few shipyards had offices, and most used the local inn for meetings with customers and contractors – and on the very rare occasions when the workforce met as a group.

Apprentices were recruited from time to time, those with small ambition being little more than cheap labour, whilst others with drive and initiative were appreciative of this opportunity to learn some of the skills of the Master. Signed indentures bound them to stringent conditions for several

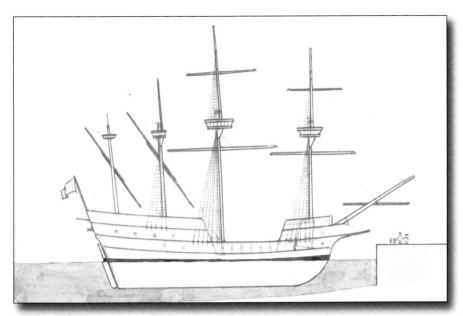

The galleasse Grand Mistress *was one of the largest ships built at Smallhythe (in 1545) and a sophisticated vessel for her time. This sketch, showing the Master Shipwright, his wife and two grandchildren on the quayside gives an indication of the great size of some of the 16th century ships*

years, and extracted a promise of non-disclosure to others regarding the "mysteries" of the Shipwrights' Trade. In a medieval industry where skill levels were not of the highest – mystique was a means of maintaining a good social and financial position.

The shipbuilders

Up to the middle of the 18th century, the vast bulk of shipbuilders were itinerant workers who in those times of privation, moved along the coast between sites as work became available. Although most were unlettered, they were proud of their skills as shipwrights and jealous of their rights to enjoy the relative freedom of working on ship hulls; they were "their own men". To this day groups of men continue to work in teams, often with long-term links brought about by friendship and family connections, like the shipwrights from Australia, Denmark, Germany, New Zealand, North America, the UK and other countries who travel the world to build replica sailing ships and other wooden vessels.

While it is impractical to build a sea-going hull with a team of two men, a boy and a dog, equally it is remarkable just how much work can be completed by a couple of dozen motivated men in just a few months. The principal team members are Shipwrights (sometimes called Carpenters), men skilled in preparing, erecting and completing all the woodwork. They would work with their own small hand tools, kept sharp and in immaculate order and would be assisted by Apprentices, bound by indenture for something like five years, and working for derisory wages, and also by Scavelmen (semi-skilled waterfront workers) and Labourers (or helpers) for the heavy and less skilled parts of the work.

Ancillary workers in the shipbuilding organisation

The many and complex tasks in the shipbuilding process required skilled ancillary workers. Some would be on the pay-roll of the Master Shipwright, whilst others would be working on a sub-contract basis. They included:

The **Sawyers**, whose task was to cut the raw lumber into planks or other required shapes for immediate use by the shipwrights. With the introduction in the 12th and 13th centuries of efficient, long, two-handed saws, the old trade of

Timber Cleaver became redundant; the cleavers' task had been to split tree trunks lengthwise using axes, wedges and sledge hammers. This was a time-consuming practice, but one that had been perfected by the Vikings a few hundred years earlier.

The **Spar Maker**, whose task was to construct masts and spars for the new ship: often not part of the shipyard organisation, but a person working closely with the Master Shipwright to ensure that the costly masts and spars were correct in size, shape and detail.

Another group allied to the shipwright's trade were the **Riggers**. Their task was to prepare and fit the standing rigging of the ship, the fixed stays and shrouds keeping the masts and bowsprit in place. Once the masts were positioned, the riggers arranged the running rigging – the halyards, sheets and lifts which enabled the crew to work the ship. Closely associated with rigging was the work of the **Sailmaker**, usually an independent trader who purchased canvas in rolls for cutting and stitching to the required shape.

Ropemakers and **Canvas Manufacturers** were essential trades, although owing to their high capital requirements, were found in urban areas and seldom in small shipbuilding towns.

The **Blacksmith** was an important person in shipbuilding communities like Smallhythe. At his forge, the fasteners for the hull planking – the nails, dumps and so on – were hand-forged. The use of iron was developing in the 1400s and shipbuilding was enhanced with its use. Blacksmiths often worked on a sub-contract basis to the Master Shipwright.

Iron Founders in medieval times were dependent on supplies of iron ore and charcoal. The iron used at Smallhythe came from smelters in various parts of the south of England, whilst the charcoal was manufactured by **Charcoal Burners** working in many parts of the Weald of Kent. Charcoal, rich in carbon, is the residue of timber heated within an enclosed earth dome and in near oxygen free conditions for about five days. Both the south of England and many parts of central Europe were significantly deforested by this process which continued well into the 20th century. Charcoal burners were never part of any shipbuilding organisation, but sold their product directly to smelters, blacksmiths and others.

The principal raw material for the shipyards was timber, and the suppliers were landowners and farmers in Kent and Sussex and possibly even further afield. Suitable shipbuilding timbers had to be chosen on site, felled and cleaned of branches before being transported to Smallhythe by ox or horse-drawn waggons. This was done by the last group in the extended shipbuilding family, **Foresters** and **Drivers**.

The entire shipbuilding staff worked long hours, usually from dawn to sunset over a six-day working week. Unless special arrangements had been agreed, most men worked for a daily sum of a few pennies. There were no first aid facilities and there was no compensation for accidents in the workplace which could be serious, if not fatal. Most injuries were caused by saws, axes, adzes and other hand tools, but some by falls or by objects falling from a height in the yard.

A health hazard singular to the area in earlier times was Marsh Fever, a form of Malaria carried by two types of mosquito found in Kent and East Sussex. After 1600 the disease became more prevalent when the amount of brackish or sea water declined, and an increased number of stagnant fresh water pools were able to host the mosquito larvae.

The customers

The vast bulk of contracts at Smallhythe were for small vessels, and it is certain that orders for Royal ships would not have been forthcoming until the quality of work and standards of supervision had been established. Small fishing smacks, local ferries and small barges would have been part of their early workload and as time progressed more prestigious work came their way – including, in 1400, a barge for the town of New Romney, paid from civic funds. It is known that vessels came to Smallhythe for major rebuilds, while others on the river for trade used the facilities for voyage repairs. Payment systems must have been quite involved and would have included both straight financial transactions (possibly in different currencies) as well as part payment by goods and services.

Ship types

There is no record of Smallhythe specialising in a particular type of ship, but the vessels generally built in southern England 500 years ago included:

Barges were the basic workhorses and seldom exceeded 50 tons. They had to be "worked" by sweeps, that is long oars, but many had one or two masts and could be sailed in suitable conditions. They were the precursor of the ubiquitous 19th century Thames Barge.

Balingers were vastly upgraded barges, with up to three masts and could carry cargo of up to 100 tonnes deadweight on continental voyages. The balinger was a near relative to the North European Cog, which was the main cargo ship used in the Hanseatic trade.

Pinnaces were small, fast sailing craft, able to make short sea passages: often they acted as tenders to larger ships such as galleasses. Most pinnaces had two masts and seldom were much longer than 14 metres on the waterline. One significant pinnace – the *Virginia* built in North America in 1608 to recognisable English design – is known to have crossed the Atlantic three times.

Great Ships also known as **Ships** and sometimes as **Carracks** were the largest vessels of up to 1,000 tons and with three or four masts. The two after masts, the Mizzen and the Bonaventure, usually were rigged with lateen sails.

Galleasses were similar to Ships and in addition to their sails were equipped with long oars or sweeps. This enabled them to manoeuvre round pure sailing craft when in action. The working of the sweeps on the decks was found to be a hindrance and by 1550 all had been rebuilt as Ships.

Typical of small ships built in the 1500s, the Pinnace was a fast and seaworthy workboat often used as a tender to larger ships. One pinnace - the Virginia *(1607) built by an English shipwright in Maine - has the distinction of being (probably) the first ship built in North America and also of having crossed the Atlantic three times*

15th Century Merchantman

The naval arms race

It was fortunate that Smallhythe was well established when King Henry VIII decided that a small fleet of ships should be assembled – all dedicated to his direct service, or in modern parlance, ships for the defence of the realm. Prior to that, any invasion fleets or similar expeditions were dependent on suitable merchant ships being available for charter (being taken up from trade) or being requisitioned from dependable sources like the Cinque Ports as part of their contractual obligations to the Crown.

In the 15th century, most ships operating for the King were used as transports and the warship had not developed as a dedicated ship type. Very few warships had heavy guns mounted aboard, and their main offensive attributes were high-towered castles both fore and aft which were manned by archers and by soldiers who were trained to leap from one ship to another during close encounters. Most had platforms about half way up each mast, known as fighting tops, where skilled marksmen and the best of the archers were positioned to pick off any enemy crew involved in hand-to-hand fighting on the open decks below.

On the death of King Henry VII in 1509, England had enjoyed peace for some years and the political landscape seemed reasonably settled with France. The thrones of England and Scotland were occupied by Henry VIII and James IV – brothers-in-law who were manipulating their relationships with great care as both royal families, the Tudors and the Stuarts, had aspirations to inherit the British throne.

At that time, Scotland had a number of good ships and might have been described as a small but efficient maritime nation. King James IV, a multilingual polymath, was not slow to appreciate how new methods of construction would enable larger and more efficient ships to be built - ships with wide decks, great structural strength and ballasted correctly to carry modern guns. A ship of 1,000 tons was built on the banks of the River Forth. Known as the *Michael*, she was the largest ship in the world and the most revolutionary, and all at a time when it was widely known that the gun foundry in Edinburgh Castle was carrying out experimental work on weapons for use at sea.

The new King of England, Henry VIII, until then little interested in political or scientific change, took notice that England was being left behind in an arms race dominated by other European countries. He oversaw the build-up of his own fleet with ships ordered from the Thames, from the newly established Royal Dockyards and from Smallhythe. It is probable that the first deliveries of his reign from Smallhythe were the *Great Bark* and the *Lesser Bark*, both of 1515.

The two fledgling naval services of England and Scotland were the precursors of the later united British fleet that just after the Restoration of the monarchy (1660) was to be given a proud appellation: *The Royal Navy*.

Ship design

Ship design has evolved over 3,000 years – initially a gradual process relying on the empirical observations of master shipwrights and master mariners. Over the medieval period ships gained in size, their carrying capacity improved, they became just a little safer and shipwrights began to have some (very small) understanding of stability, or the means of keeping vessels upright. As ship plans did not exist before 1600, all the ships constructed at Smallhythe were "built by eye" under the close superintendence of the Master Shipwright, who would have his private guidance notes on the proportions of the hull cross sections and other matters – part of the mystery of the profession alluded to earlier.

From earliest times ship layout has been fairly standard irrespective of the country of construction. This was the result of the international dimensions of shipping, ship-handling and shipbuilding – businesses manned by personnel from every part of Europe. An example of this is

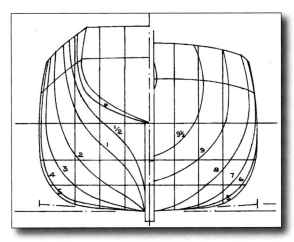

Smallhythe ships were built well before the time of plans drawn on paper. Despite this we have been able to generate the body plan of one of the Great Ships. Eleven cross sections are used traditionally to define the shape of the hull, with the fore end of the hull to the right and the after end to the left

the established order of securing rope and cordage on the deck, enabling professional multi-national crews, despite their linguistic problems, to react promptly and in unison during an emergency.

Construction on site

It is probable that two differing methods of construction were used at Smallhythe. In the very earliest years, a cradle forming the ship's shape would have been built, into which the outer shell planks would have been laid (overlapping each other and in clinker format) and secured with nails or droves. Then the frames (the ribs of the ship) would be offered up and the hull formed. In early medieval times this system fell out of favour in Europe, although it remains in use to this day in parts of South East Asia.

Most Smallhythe ships were built using the frame-first system, where a keel was laid down on building blocks. The keel was a key part of the structure and was preferably a single length of timber, but if only shorter timbers were available, the keel was fabricated from the best available and the parts bolted together at complex scarf joints. The ship frames were set vertically and at right angles to the keel line and then secured by the keelson, by the deck beams and by stringers. At

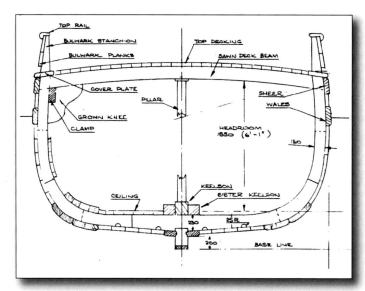

An analysis of the mid-section of a 16th century pinnace showing the complexity and the mass of wooden ship construction

carried out on the shoulders of the building team, all protected by leathers, placed on the hull, bent to shape and secured. On cooling, the timber would set permanently in its new shape. The hull integrity was completed with the laying of decks, formed of long planks pointing fore and aft and fitted such that the sheer (the fore and aft curvature) of the deck and the camber (the transverse round) of the deck was allowed for.

As a hull was built of hundreds of component timber parts, the fasteners were items of great importance. Many were iron nails, droves and bolts, but the most intriguing were Treenails, often described as Trunnels which joined large timbers together – as shown in the sketch.

this stage the ship was "in frame" and the hull shape was apparent. The frames were prefabricated using carefully sawn timber parts which were bolted together.

The hull or shell planking had to be prepared with great care as each plank was curved in two directions and had to be cut and bevelled before being subjected to heat in a steam box. Once they had reached 100° Celsius, the long planks were

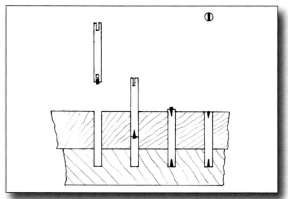

A timber dowel of strong and dense timber used to join large timber members in a ship; usually described as a Trunnel. At each end is a slot with a tapered wedge, making a rock-hard fastener capable of lasting more than 100 years

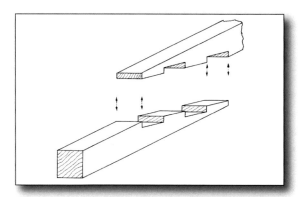

The key part of the ship's structure is the keel – normally of Oak (Quercus robur) and it is a timber that in a perfect world should be one undivided piece. Demands on the forests of south England over centuries, has made finding pieces longer than 30 metres difficult. The shipwrights have overcome this problem by scarfing keel joints: in large ships the scarfs are more complex than shown here

Apart from hand tools, the major implements used would have been a saw-pit where two men worked double-ended saws (see page 24), the steam box of very simple design and a sheerlegs – a lifting device set up by the riggers using spars.

Ships were built bow to the water with the stern higher up. This allowed the strong stern post to be the point of attachment for the lines that would force the ship down greased wooden rails at the time of launch. Launching required considerable physical effort as it would be a couple of centuries before dynamic launching was evolved and ships slipped into the water under their own weight.

Once afloat, the ship would be ballasted with large smooth stones arranged to be supported on the frame structure and fastened to avoid movement in rough weather. The lower masts might have been fitted and some outfitting, including a stone galley hearth for cooking, completed. After a few weeks the new ship would have been part rowed and part towed to Winchelsea or some other coastal port to have heavy items like guns fitted, and then be prepared for the first sea voyage.

Building a ship is one of the world's most rewarding tasks, and an exciting part is the final handover of the new rigged ship, ready for sea!

View of a modern ship with after frames in process of erection

Tonnage

Tonnage is a convenient method of describing the size – or the magnitude – of a ship. It does not refer to the mass or weight of the ship, but rather the carrying capacity of the hull. In the 12th or 13th centuries, one of the major imports to our islands was wine from France and as this trade had to be regulated, it was necessary to estimate the capacity of ships. Around the 1420s, it was enacted that wine containers (known as tuns) be of at least 252 gallons and from then on they were largely standardised and ships were known as having a capacity of so many tuns, a figure upon which port charges and taxes were paid. By sheer coincidence the mass or weight of a tun of wine was close to the mass of one long (UK) ton of 2,240 lb.

As ship design was quite elementary, the authorities decided that for taxation and port-due purposes ships would have to be measured for tonnage – confirming it as a capacity matter.

Until the 19th century ship tonnage was based on variations of the formula:

Tonnage = (**L** x **B** x **D**) / 94

Where **L**   is the length of keel of the ship in feet
   B   is the breadth of the ship (inside planking) and again in feet
   D   is the depth of the ship from the top of the keel to the underside of deck at midships and once again in feet

While not perfect it gave a means for comparing the relative carrying capacities of different ships.

Today, in the 21st century, international regulations require ships to be measured for gross and for net tonnages – all based on the capacity of the ship. The "weight" or mass of the ship is the displacement stated in metric tonnes and the cargo-carrying capacity is known as deadweight and again is measured in metric tonnes.

Models of ships have hung in churches since medieval times. Often known as votive models, they may express the gratitude of a family for the return of their dearest ones from a perilous voyage, or sometimes serve as memorials to a fine crew lost at sea. Denmark (where every church is within 40 miles of the sea) has over 800 ship models, known there as Kirkeskiber – similar to the Scottish name Kirk Ships. Since the Second World War, there has been renewed interest in church ships and many more models are now found throughout Britain – pride of place going to the lovely London church of All Hallows-by-the-Tower, where about a dozen fine models are on display along with many other fascinating maritime relics.

Some years ago, as interest in Smallhythe shipbuilding was reviving, a member of the congregation at St Mildred's Church, Tenterden offered to pay for a votive model of one of the Smallhythe Fleet to hang in the building.

The ship chosen was the galleasse *Grand Mistress* built at Smallhythe in 1545. The design was prepared by the author of this chapter using "reverse engineering" techniques and then the model was constructed by a distinguished model maker on the staff of the National Maritime Museum, Greenwich. The beautiful model hangs today at the west end of the nave of St Mildred's.

Some ships known to have been built at Smallhythe

Year	Name	Type	Tonnage	Notes
1364	*La Gabriel*	barge?		
1378	*La Seint Marie*	barge?		
1394	*Marie*		100 tons	
1400	*St Eneswythe*	barge		for New Romney
1410	*Marie*	barge	100 tons	
1416	*Jesus*	ship	1,000 tons	
1416	*George*	balinger	120 tons	
1486	*Regent*	ship	600 tons	built at Reading?
1497	*Mary Fortune*		80 tons	
1515	*Great Bark*			
1515	*Lesser Bark*			
1545	*Grand Mistress*	galleasse	450 tons	
1545	*Anne Gallant*	galleasse	450 tons	built at Reading?
1546	*Great Gallyon*	ship	300 tons	
?	*Lesser Gallyon*	ship	200 tons	built at Reading?

The Embarkation of Henry VIII at Dover *c.1520-40.*
The painting marks the departure of Henry VIII and his fleet for Calais on 31 May 1520 on the way to meet Francis I at the Field of the Cloth of Gold. Among the ships is the Henri Grace a Dieu, *built in Woolwich with the aid of men and timber from Smallhythe*

CHAPTER 3

Smallhythe and the Cinque Ports

Maurice Dalton

Ever since Roman times, the south-east of England faced the threat of invaders or raiding pirates. The most successful response to these threats was the concept of "Ship Service" and eventually the creation of the Cinque Ports Confederation, a network of ports in Kent and Sussex that were prepared to supply ships and men to defend the English Channel coast and, indeed, the country. Smallhythe was brought within the ambit of the Cinque Ports in 1449 when the Hundred[1] of Tenterden, which included Smallhythe, agreed to assist the Cinque Port of Rye with its obligation to supply ships and crews to the monarch for the defence of the realm. Tenterden's decision to respond positively to a plea from Rye for assistance was not just for good neighbour relations. With the commitment to supply the ships and men came significant local and national privileges and immunities.

Origin of the Cinque Ports

The precise origin of the Confederation is unclear. Although some historians have suggested that the Cinque Ports had their roots in a chain of coastal forts, possibly founded by Emperor Constantine I early in the 4th century AD, the generally accepted view is that it was the Saxon Kings of England, during the 11th century, who first formalised the arrangement under which key coastal towns in Kent and Sussex were offered inducements to provide the monarch with ships and men, in place of the mercenary vessels relied upon by their predecessors.

It is probable that Edward the Confessor, who reigned from 1042 to 1066, was the first monarch to deploy a fleet of ships to defend the English Channel. Up to this time fishing boat owners in the South East had been pressed into putting their vessels and crews at the disposal of the monarch, either to defend the nation at home or to pursue his interests overseas. The new arrangements between monarch and port were set out in Royal Charters granted over several centuries and it is clear from the terms of these charters and from other evidence, including the *Pipe Rolls* of Henry II and from the *Domesday Book* (published in 1086), that the ports had enjoyed common privileges in return for their service to the Crown since the 11th century and were by that time already known collectively as the Cinque Ports.

The Cinque Ports were of immense importance to England in the Middle Ages, when they were the main line of defence against foreign invaders. Although the increasing need to convey people and armies across the Channel and occasionally to fight battles at sea imposed a significant and

[1] A division of a county for military and judicial purposes

growing burden on the ship owners of the South East, they rose to the challenge and the unique collaboration between English Channel ports served the country well for 400 years, from the 12th to the 16th centuries. It also provided the foundation upon which Britain built the Royal Navy and became a world-dominating maritime power between the 17th and 19th centuries.

Membership

The Cinque Ports Confederation takes its name from the Norman French word for "five", the number of ports in the South East of England that originally put their ships at the disposal of the monarch, in an arrangement known as "Ship Service". "Cinque" is pronounced not as a French word but as the English word "sink". The five ports, known as the "Head Ports", from west to east were Hastings, Romney, Hythe, Dover and Sandwich. The obligations placed on the five relatively small fishing communities became a heavy burden and the head ports looked to neighbouring towns and villages for help in providing ships, equipment and men. For example, Hastings turned to the ports of Rye and Winchelsea to help it deliver its quota of ships and men and in 1189 the two ports became "limbs" of Hastings. During the 13th century,

they went from contributing just two ships between them to providing a total of 15 out of Hastings' quota of 21. In 1336 Rye and Winchelsea were both formally recognised as full members of the Confederation in their own right. They were referred to as the "Two Ancient Towns" rather than "head ports" necessitating a change in the name of the Confederation to "The Cinque Ports and the Two Ancient Towns".

Royal Charters

The arrangements between monarch and port were promulgated in Royal Charters which were granted to individual ports or collectively to the Confederation. The earliest known charter to the Cinque Ports collectively (a *general charter*) was granted by King Henry III in 1260. A general charter was widely regarded as less effective than charters granted to individual towns, and the ports continued to seek their own individual charters long after the first collective grants were made. A century earlier, in 1155-56, Henry II had granted similar individual charters to at least three of the head ports, probably to secure the ships which he needed in connection with a visit to Normandy (which was part of his realm at that time) and for his planned conquest of Ireland.

The five Head Ports and two Ancient Towns of the Cinque Ports

Smallhythe – From Ships to Sheep

Cinque Ports Arms

The arms of the Cinque Ports (shown below), symbolise the ports' ship service to the Crown by joining the front half of three lions of England with the rear half of three ships. This heraldic device almost certainly originated between about 1194 – when *three lions passant guardant* were adopted as the arms of English kings – and 1305 when the ports' arms were featured on a common seal used by the town of Dover. It is impossible to date the granting of the arms precisely, but there is some evidence to suggest that they were granted by Edward I, in the final decade of the 13th century.

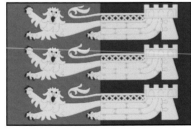

The Arms of English kings (top) and the Cinque Ports

Obligations and Benefits

Henry II's charters granted the ports significant benefits in exchange for the ports providing a specified number of ships, each with a crew of 21 men and a boy, for 15 days' service to the king, annually. If their service was required for longer than 15 days in any year, the ports were entitled to payment for the additional period. Initially, Hastings and Dover furnished 20 fully manned ships each and the other three ports supplied five each but by 1278 the Hastings and Dover requirement was increased to 21 ships each, making a total of 57 ships for all five ports. This obligation continued until the 16th century. The benefits granted in the Charters included the right to bring goods into the country without paying import duties as well as a range of other exemptions and benefits as shown in the panel overleaf.

There were also benefits that varied over time and from port to port, according to the particular charter. The privileges and immunities most commonly granted were:-

- Freedom from pleading 'otherwise than as the barons of ... the Cinque Ports plead', that is to say, in their own courts of law.
- Freedom from a wide range of taxes which were payable in the course of travel and trade during medieval times; including *custom, toll, lestage, passage, rivage and sponsage*.
- Freedom from *fifteenths* and *tenths* (national taxes levied by the Crown).
- The right of *withernam* which gave Portsmen (freemen of a Cinque Port) the right to pursue and enforce payment of debts through their own courts. If a Portsman was owed a debt by a resident of another town or if he was unjustly charged a toll or levy elsewhere; a warning letter would be sent to the offending town demanding payment or re-payment within 15 days. If redress was not forthcoming, the next visitor from that town would be arrested and, after a hearing, sent home with notice of the judgement against his townspeople. If that failed, the next traveller from the defaulting town was liable to be detained and his goods confiscated and sold to cover the outstanding amount.

General Privileges of the Cinque Ports

◆ Exemption from tax and tallage,
◆ Right of
  ● soc and sac, tol and team, blodwit and fledwit,
  ● pillory and tumbril,
  ● infrangentheof and outfrangentheof,
  ● mundbryce,
  ● waifs and strays,
  ● flotsam and jetsam and
  ● ligan

That is
◆ Exemption from tax and tolls
◆ Right to
  ● self-government; levy tolls, punish those who shed blood or flee justice;
  ● punish minor offences;
  ● detain and execute criminals both inside and outside the port's jurisdiction;
  ● break into or violate a man's mund or property in order to erect banks or dykes as a defence against the sea;
  ● punish breaches of the peace; possession of lost goods that remain unclaimed after a year;
  ● goods thrown overboard and floating wreckage;
  ● goods or wreckage on the seabed attached to a buoy to assist recovery

The five Head Ports and two Ancient Towns were entitled to send two representatives to sit in Parliament and to send representatives, known as Coronation Barons, to attend upon monarchs at their Coronation ceremonies[2].

There were also disadvantages to membership of the Confederation, mostly financial. In times of hardship, a port's commitment weighed heavily on the townsfolk. At other times there were simply disputes as to how the burden should be split. When Tenterden became a limb of Rye in 1449, it had to take on a share of Rye's obligations. A long-running disagreement between them as to the division of those obligations was only finally resolved in the 1760s when Rye unsuccessfully brought a suit against Tenterden for the non-payment of the annual contribution towards ship service that Rye deemed appropriate.

[2] See page 41

Smallhythe and the Cinque Ports

Smallhythe never became a member of the Cinque Ports in its own right. Despite the constant presence of ships, and of men who could man them, Smallhythe does not appear to have had any form of relationship with the Cinque Ports before 1449. Most likely this was because Smallhythe was "inland", did not maintain a standing fishing fleet and therefore was not in a position to supply vessels and men to the monarch. When a connection was eventually established, it was to be through its larger neighbour Tenterden.

By the mid-15th century, Rye, seven miles to the south of Smallhythe, had become impoverished by years of destructive enemy attacks, coastal raiders and silting-up of the port, and could no longer meet its obligations as a Cinque Port. Tenterden, on the other hand, just three miles to the north of Smallhythe, had grown rich from cloth-making. Edward III in the 1330s had encouraged Flemish cloth workers to bring their skills to this country and Kent became a centre of broadcloth production. In Tenterden, wool from sheep farmed on the Romney Marsh was spun and woven into woollen broadcloth that had a reputation for durability, good mix and colour. The industry brought wealth to several families in Tenterden who added much to the prosperity of the town. Exports of cloth were conducted through the port at Smallhythe, situated just within the southern boundary of the Hundred of Tenterden.

When beleaguered Rye sought help from its rich neighbour, Tenterden agreed to help by providing one of Rye's quota of ships and a crew of 24 men, as well as a yearly sum of 6 marks (£4) and a contribution towards the cost of the Confederation's courts. In exchange, the Hundred of Tenterden became a member of the Confederation, as a limb of Rye, and enjoyed all of the considerable benefits of membership. The agreement was sealed by Henry VI who on 1 August 1449 granted Tenterden its first Royal Charter. The Charter effectively separated Tenterden (and Smallhythe) from the County of Kent and allowed the town to manage most of its own affairs.

Smallhythe – From Ships to Sheep

At the time that Tenterden with Smallhythe joined the Confederation, the original Cinque Ports had been in existence for about 300 years and no doubt the new members felt that the special status that they had acquired through membership as a limb of Rye would continue indefinitely. In fact within the next century it would become obvious that the Cinque Ports were unable to keep pace with the increasing demands of the monarch and the country for bigger and more specialised vessels and, consequently, the erstwhile justification for their special privileges and immunities was in danger of falling away.

Challenges and Decline

Early naval engagements usually consisted of ramming and/or boarding opposing vessels, but changing methods of naval warfare and especially the introduction of naval artillery led to the need for ever larger ships. From the 14th century, the Cinque Ports were allowed to provide fewer ships on condition that each was manned by a crew of 42 and was capable of carrying double the amount of goods and equipment than hitherto. Some members of the Confederation struggled to cope with these developments and their inability to supply larger and more specialised ships and crews would eventually lead to a decline in the power and influence of the Cinque Ports Confederation. From the time of the Confederation's creation, the Cinque Ports had also faced other challenges to their existence, not least from the effects of the constantly changing coastline, brought about by the ravages of the sea. In the latter part of the 13th century the south-east coast was devastated by a series of severe storms, culminating in the Great Storm of 1287, which weakened the coastal defences of the Romney Marsh, permanently changed the coastline and made some harbours unusable.

In the 16th century, a number of events taken together spelt the end of the role of the Cinque Ports. The development of royal dockyards at Chatham and Portsmouth, as well as the growth of London, Gravesend, Southampton and Plymouth as safe ports, and the creation of a permanent Navy by Henry VIII, coincided with a general decline in the ability of the Cinque Ports to provide the type of ship and quantity of men required by the monarch. At the same time the Crown was becoming more involved in national government, and was not disposed towards the semi-independent status of the members of the Confederation. Faced with these developments, the Cinque Ports had no alternative but to accept that their day was coming to an end. Eventually, the move from fishing vessels to purpose-built warships such as the *Mary Rose*, launched in 1510, and the growing size of these warships, rendered obsolete the vessels of the Cinque Ports.

By the reign of Queen Elizabeth I, the Cinque Ports had effectively ceased to be of any real significance. Having been called upon to supply ships and men in 1588 to help defend the country against the Spanish Armada, the last recorded occasion on which Cinque Ports vessels saw action was in 1596, when the Spanish again threatened to invade England, and five Cinque Ports ships joined the English fleet in its pre-emptive raid on Cadiz.

With its role in the defence of the nation over, the Confederation lost its influence and power. The individual ports lost their unique privileges and immunities and were gradually absorbed back into the general administration of the country. Local Government reforms and Acts of Parliament passed during the 19th and 20th centuries (notably the Great Reform Act of 1832) extinguished the remaining administrative and judicial powers of the Confederation of the Cinque Ports.

Despite the loss of power and influence, the member towns still jealously guard the customs, traditions and the few remaining rights and privileges of their ancient organisation, such as the attendance of Cinque Ports Barons at the Coronations of British monarchs.

Aspects of the Cinque Ports

Lord Warden of the Cinque Ports

The office of Lord Warden of the Cinque Ports was established by King Edward I in his Great Charter of 1278 to provide central authority and control over the Portsmen and to act as a link between their interests and the Crown. For centuries it was one of the most powerful and important positions in the country. Originally known as the Keeper of the Coast, the office is one of the oldest appointments in the world. The role of the Lord Warden was to maintain the strategic defences of south-eastern England and to act as the link between the

Queen Elizabeth The Queen Mother,
Lord Warden of the Cinque Ports 1978-2002

Crown and the Cinque Ports, a key element of those defences. He was also responsible for the return of writs, including parliamentary writs of summons, and performing the other duties of a sheriff. His powers were considerable, for he also had authority over Dover Castle (as Constable of the Castle) and over the Crown's other coastal

fortifications in the region; and exercised admiralty jurisdiction from Dungeness in Kent to the Naze in Essex. The Keeper of the Coast, instituted in the mid-11th century, was hereditary until the reign of Richard I, after which the office was filled by royal appointees.

The successor office of Lord Warden still exists but is now largely ceremonial. The office-holder is still appointed by the monarch, usually in recognition of distinguished service to the country. The Lord Warden is supported by a small staff and has the use of an official residence at Walmer Castle. In the past century or two, the position of Lord Warden has been held by a number of well-known figures, including William Pitt the Younger (1792), The Duke of Wellington (1829), Sir Winston Churchill (1941) and Queen Elizabeth The Queen Mother (1978). The Queen Mother held the appointment up to her death in 2002 and is the only woman to have been appointed to the office. Her successor as Lord Warden was Admiral the Lord Boyce, a former Chief of the Defence Staff, who was appointed in December 2004.

Representation in Parliament

All freemen of the five Head Ports and the two Ancient Towns, known as "Portsmen", were deemed to be barons, and thus entitled to attend parliament. Those selected to attend parliament were termed "Barons of the Cinque Ports" and took precedence over representatives of the shires and boroughs. Writs of summons to parliament were sent to the Lord Warden following which representative Barons of the Cinque Ports were selected to attend parliament. This privilege did not extend to the members of the Confederation that were "limbs" of the Head Ports and Ancient Towns.

Honours at Court

Among the privileges conferred on the Cinque Ports, the barons of the five Head Ports and two Ancient Towns were granted the right of "Honours at Court". These included the right to attend the monarch at his or her coronation in Westminster Abbey and, in common with the citizens of London, Oxford and Canterbury, to perform specific tasks during the ceremonies. In the barons' case, they had the duty of supplying and carrying ornate canopies over the head of the king and, when married, over the head of his queen, during their processions between Westminster Hall in the Palace of Westminster (today part of the Houses of Parliament) and Westminster Abbey before and after the coronation ceremony, as a symbol of the role that they played in defending king and country. At the coronation banquet in Westminster Hall that followed the ceremony, the barons were entitled to sit at the table to the right of the king and queen. After the ceremony the barons were also entitled to claim the canopies as a perquisite of their role in the procession.

The first occasion on which the barons of the Cinque Ports carried a canopy over the head of the monarch was the Coronation of Richard the Lionheart in 1189. The canopy was an elaborate affair. The Custumal of Rye records that

"of all the [Cinque] Ports there must come thirty two barons all in one clothing, and they shall bear the cloth over the king and over the queen, with four spears, of the colour silver, and four little bells gilt, having about the cloth, which is called the fall and shall come from the King's Treasury".

In subsequent coronations up to that of George IV, the barons continued to carry a canopy over the king and queen. An anonymous account of the Coronation of King George IV in 1821 noted that the canopy was

"yellow – of silk and gold embroidery, with short curtains of muslin spangle with gold" and that *"it was held aloft on eight steel poles with silver knobs".*

These arrangements did not always go without incident. There seems to have been some rivalry or perhaps jealousy at court at the time of the Coronation of King Charles II, on 23 April 1661, for at the banquet after the Coronation the King's footmen tried to seize the canopy from the barons. There was an undignified scuffle, which ended in victory for the barons and imprisonment for the footmen[3]. However, during the row, the barons' seats at the banquet were taken by bishops and judges. Thinking it would be unseemly to try to dislodge them, the barons took the next best available seats at a lower table.

Samuel Pepys recorded the incident in Westminster Hall with the King's footmen in his diary for 23 April 1661.

I observed little disorder in all this; but only the King's Footmen had got hold of the Canopy and would keep it from the Barons of the Cinque Ports; which they endeavoured to force from them again but could not do it till my Lord Duke of Albermarle caused it to be put into Sir R Pye's hand till tomorrow to be decided. The Barons had been dragged along the hall, and had lost their places at table. By a prompt command of the King, the Footmen were imprisoned and dismissed.

Pepys was himself a Baron of the Cinque Ports and represented Sandwich at the Coronation of James II.

One hundred and sixty years later, at the Coronation of King George IV in 1821, the barons again carried a canopy over the king, both during the service and afterwards for the procession to Westminster Hall. Some reports of the procession suggest that George IV decided to walk in front of the canopy so that the onlookers could have a better opportunity to see the newly crowned king. If so, this departure from the script appears not to have been

[3] *Coronation: A History of Kingship and the British Monarchy*, Roy Strong (2005)

Barons of the Cinque Ports carrying the canopy over King James I and Queen Anne
at their Coronation on 25 July 1603

communicated to the barons. Other reports record that the barons found it difficult to stop the canopy from swaying during the procession and the king, fearing for his safety, decided to walk just ahead of the canopy.

No matter which version is correct, the barons, noticing that the king was no longer under the cover of their canopy, increased their pace, causing the canopy to sway ever more vigorously.

The king, determined to remain clear of the canopy, also increased his step and the procession duly arrived at Westminster Hall almost at a trot.

The right of the Cinque Ports barons to attend coronations and carry canopies over the head of the monarch and his queen was observed without fail from the Coronation of Henry III up to that of George IV but went into abeyance

Barons of the Cinque Ports carrying the canopy over King James II and Queen Mary
at their Coronation on 23 April 1685

Smallhythe – From Ships to Sheep

after the barons' performance in 1821. In 1902, for the Coronation of King Edward VII, the right to attend coronations (but not to carry a canopy over the monarch) was revived and extended to all of the Cinque Ports, including the "limbs". Each member of the Confederation appointed a baron to attend the ceremony and the Mayor of Tenterden, Councillor The Reverend Joseph Robert Diggle, was elected as Tenterden's baron. Incidentally, Councillor Diggle's son, W Wrigley Diggle, designed the War Memorial which stands on Tenterden High Street. With the consignment of the canopy to history, in 1902 the Cinque Ports barons were given the responsibility of holding the standards of England, Scotland, Ireland and the United Kingdom after they had been processed into Westminster Abbey by standard bearers and of returning the standards to the standard bearers for the procession out of the Abbey at the end of the coronation ceremony. In 1911, the standards of the Dominions (Australia, New Zealand, Canada and South Africa) were added and in 1937 the flag of the Principality of Wales and a number of Royal standards were further added. In 1953, at the Coronation of Queen Elizabeth II, the barons held the standards of the home countries and of Commonwealth member states after they had been processed into the Abbey by representatives of the home countries and by the High Commissioners for the Commonwealth countries[4].

Tenterden's Baron in 1953 was Councillor Stanley Day, the Mayor of Tenterden at the time, and a long-time resident of Smallhythe. Although born a few miles away in Marden, in the 1930s he moved to Pickhill Farm on the Smallhythe side of the border with Tenterden where he farmed 300 acres of fruit and hops. He was a councillor at Tenterden from 1940 to 1964, elected an alderman in 1956 and was elected mayor in 1949 and again in 1953. He remained a councillor until 1964. Like all of the other Cinque Ports barons at the Coronation, he was tasked with holding one of the standards of the home and Commonwealth countries represented at the ceremony, in his case the standard of Ceylon (now Sri Lanka).

Councillor Day was also a magistrate for about 20 years and a churchwarden at Smallhythe Church as well as a member of the Kent Cricket Club, president of both Tenterden and Smallhythe cricket clubs and of Tenterden and District Horticultural Society and other local organisations. A real man of the people.

[4] Ceremonial of the Coronation of Queen Elizabeth II, published in a supplement dated 20 November 1953 to the *London Gazette* of 17 November 1953

Coronation Barons' Attire

The ceremonial dress for Barons of the Cinque Ports attending a coronation has changed somewhat over the years. At the Coronation of King James I in 1603 they wore "a scarlet gown reaching down to the ankles, citizen fashion, faced with crimson, silk stockings, crimson velvet shoes, and black velvet caps" and were each paid 14 shillings and fourpence (70p in today's currency and in cash terms equivalent to about £150) towards their expenses, the money being raised from the members of the Cinque Ports[5].

For the Coronation of King James II in 1685, the barons were similarly dressed in doublets (jackets) of crimson satin, scarlet hose, scarlet gowns lined with crimson satin, black velvet caps fastened on their sleeves, and black velvet shoes[6].

Later, up to the mid-19th century, the Barons were dressed in Jacobean-style blue and red silk satin doublets, breeches and sur-coats, worn

[5, 6] *History of the town and port of Dover and of Dover Castle* by the Rev. John Lyon

Rev. J. R. Diggle, Mayor of Tenterden and Baron of the Cinque Ports, in his Coronation Robes 1902

Since that time, the dress has remained unchanged and an example, worn in 1953 by the Mayor of Tenterden, Councillor Stanley Day, at the Coronation of Queen Elizabeth II on 2 June, is on display in Tenterden Museum.

As barons for the day of the Coronation only, it was natural for the Coronation Barons to try to make as much of the day as possible. The advent of rapid travel by train in the 19th century allowed the barons to return to their home towns on the day of the Coronation, rather than spending several days travelling to and from London. On their return they were able to join in the local celebrations, already by then well underway, proudly wearing their ceremonial robes, as the photographs of Councillor Day (opposite) show. Although late in the evening, not only was the Mayor still in the robes of a Coronation Baron but all of Tenterden's other office holders and notables were also in their ceremonial attire to greet him on his return to Tenterden.

Ceremonial dress at the Tenterden Museum

with red stockings, white kid shoes and a black hat trimmed with red and white ostrich feathers. A costume of this confection, worn by Thomas Lamb, Lord Mayor of Rye in 1808, survives in the collection at Brighton Museum & Art Gallery.

The ceremonial dress worn at the Coronation of King Edward VII in 1902 comprised a rich silk velvet coat, lined throughout with white silk, silk velvet breeches, a white silk velvet waistcoat embroidered with flowers all of the early Victorian period, lace ruffles and jabot, and a velvet cap. The robe was in scarlet cloth, lined with white silk, with blue velvet facings edged with gold lace and the bars and arms of the Cinque Ports embroidered in the right shoulder. The dress is well illustrated by Daisy Radcliff Beresford's portrait in Tenterden Town Hall of the Reverend Joseph Robert Diggle, Mayor of Tenterden and Coronation Baron in 1902.

CHAPTER 4

The Great Fire

Maurice Dalton

In September 1666 the City of London was engulfed in a Great Fire. Much is known about this devastating event; how it started, where it spread, how it was fought, which properties were destroyed and so on. There are many records, descriptions, paintings, reports and other sources of information. One hundred and fifty years earlier the nationally important shipbuilding centre of Smallhythe was also consumed by a Great Fire. Whilst it would be misleading to suggest that the two events were comparable in importance, some might find it a surprise to know that there is not a single contemporary record of the fire that swept through Smallhythe on a summer's day in the early part of the 16th century. Why are there no records of what actually happened? The answer is probably in one word – "fire". Fire was a common event and when the Court Hall in Tenterden, where it is likely that Smallhythe's records would have been sent for safe-keeping, was itself destroyed by fire on 19 March 1661, it is probable that all of Smallhythe's records were destroyed as well.

Although we cannot be sure that the fire is the reason for the absence of records, what we do know is that no contemporary records of the Great Fire of Smallhythe are known to exist anywhere. Reliance has therefore been placed on a few other sources including notes in important documents that had been copied or transcribed when they had become damaged or almost illegible through use or age. Alas, the accuracy of the transcription of one particular document appears to have led to a falsehood of some significance – the actual date of the fire.

Date of the fire

One of the local historic records that has survived, but not unscathed, is The Tenterden Municipal Record Book. Among other things, the Record Book not only records the appointment of the town's bailiffs but also includes, within the list of bailiffs, brief references to some local and national events. The document is not of one age. It was a working document to which information was added as time went by. The more or less constant use caused pages to tear, fade and crumble and parts of the original were replaced by copies. In addition, a number of transcriptions of parts of the document have also been made by researchers and others, not necessarily totally faithful to the original. One such transcription, by Robert Furley F. S. A., is a case in point.

Robert Furley, in his report *The Early History of Tenterden*, published in 1882 in the proceedings of the Kent Archaeological Society (Archaeologia

Cantiana Volume 14, page 56), noted that amongst the few records possessed by the Corporation was a minute book recording mostly local events as they happened. Within the record book was a chronological list of bailiffs of Tenterden with the occasional note of local events of importance. In a discussion about the chapel at Smallhythe, he made the following observation:

Amongst the few records possessed by the Corporation, is a minute books (sic), in which passing events appear to have been entered in chronological order. Here we find this entry: "6 Henry VIII [A.D. 1514-15], the which year Smalithe was burnt on the last day of July."

Dating of events by reference to the year of the monarch's reign was the usual method of dating official documents and records. Furley began his extract "6 Henry VIII", meaning the 6th year of Henry VIII's reign. Henry acceded to the throne on 21 April 1509 and, therefore, the 6th year of his reign began on 21 April 1514. Consequently, it had long been accepted that the fire occurred on 31 July 1514 and it was on this basis that events were held in Smallhythe in 2014 to commemorate the 500th anniversary of the fire.

However, after the commemorations had started, Mrs Mary Adams, a local historian, drew to the attention of the *Kentish Express*, the local weekly newspaper, her discovery of another version of the list of bailiffs of Tenterden. This other version of the list, she said, showed the name of each bailiff of Tenterden appointed during each monarch's reign. This was subtly different from the impression created by Furley that the list was of bailiffs in office from the commencement of each monarch's reign. Furley's interpretation, Adams maintained, took no account of the fact that bailiffs of Tenterden took office not at the beginning of the year or on the monarch's accession but on 29 August.

Further research revealed a complete list of bailiffs recorded in a paper by A H Taylor entitled *The Municipal Records of Tenterden, Part 1* which was published in the proceedings of the Kent Archaeological Society in 1917 (Archaeologia Cantiana Volume 32, page 296).

The list, Taylor said, was based on one prepared in 1558 to which additions had been made up to 1632 when a fresh version was made by Edward Boys, a freeman of Tenterden, and carried on by others. This list differed from Furley's in that it is a list of bailiffs *appointed* during each reign, not a list of bailiffs who *served* during each reign. Taylor's transcription of the pertinent part of the list reads:

296   THE MUNICIPAL RECORDS OF TENTERDEN.

secundo	William Preston	xvº	John Parker
tertio	Thomas Pette	xvjº	George ffowle
quarto	Thomas Carpenter	xvijº	Thomas Woodd dieth
quinto	Thomas Pette		& George ffowle
sexto	William Deye		s'ved
	(Davy)	xviijº	John Parker
septimo	Robert Brickenden	xixº	Thomas Asherenden
octavo	Hughe Parker	xxº	Thomas Iselande
nono	Hughe Parker		dieth & Thomas
decimo	Robert Davy dieth		Asherinden s'ved
	& Hughe Parker	xxjº	Thomas Austen
	serveth	xxijº	John Baker[12]
undecimo	Thomas Carpenter	xxiijº	John Austen
xijº	John Brickenden	xxiiijº	John Parker
xiijº	John Rogers	xxvº	John Woode
xiiijº	William Browning	xxvjº	William Brikenden
xvº	Richard Widerden	xxvijº	John Fowle the yongʳ
	dieth & William	xxviijº	John Brickenden,
	Browning s'veth		junior
xvjº	Moyses Pette	xxixº	John Austen th'elder
xvijº	Moyses Pette		[This yere yᵉ xxviij of Auguste
xviijº	John Hoigges		Kinge Henry viij came to Ten-
xixº	John Hoigges		terden.]
vicesimo	John Hales		
xxjº	John Roger	xxxº	Edward ffelippe
xxijº	William Brickenden	xxxjº	John ffowle ye yong-
xxiijº	Henry Adam		ger
xxiiijº	Edward ffelipp	xxxijº	John Austen th'elder
The yere of the reigne of			dieth & John Fowle
Kinge Henrye VIII.			s'ved
primo	John Gage, esqre[8]	xxxiijº	John Parker
[Sharley More made.]		xxxiiijº	George ffelipp
		xxxvº	Richard Aleock[13]
ijº	John Gage, esquier		[This yeare Bolen won.]
iijº	John Donett	xxxvjº	Edward Hales
iiijº	John Hoigges[9]	xxxvijº	Edward Hales
vº	John Hoigges	xxxviijº	George ffelipp
vjº	Barthelmewe ffowle	The yere of Kinge Edwarde VI.	
[The which yere Smalithe was		primo	Edward Hales
burnte on the last day of Julye.]		ijº	John Brickenden
		iijº	William Gerveis
vijº	Barthel' ffowle	iiijº	William Gerveis
octavo	William Brickenden	vº	John Woodd
nono	Robert Brickenden	sexto	Thomas Austen
deci'	Robert Brickenden	vijº	Peter Shorte
xjº	Thomas Woodd	Tempore Mariæ.	
xijº	Edward ffelipp[10]		
xiijº	Edward ffelipp	primo	Peter Shorte
xiiijº	John Parker[11]	[Hoc anno surraxit Wyatt.]	

The yere of the reigne of Kinge Henrye VIII.

primo	John Gage, esqre[8]
[Sharley More made.]	
ijº	John Gage, esquier
iijº	John Donett
iiijº	John Hoigges[9]
vº	John Hoigges
vjº	Barthelmewe ffowle
[The which yere Smalithe was burnte on the last day of Julye.]	
vijº	Barthel' ffowle

Unlike in Furley's brief quote, there were no year dates in Taylor's extensive transcription. Taylor is unlikely to have deliberately excluded this information and it is therefore reasonable to regard his text as authentic and to deduce that Barthelmewe ffowle was the 6th bailiff to be appointed *after* Henry VIII came to the throne in April 1509. As the bailiffs of Tenterden took office on 29 August each year, Barthelmewe ffowle would have taken office on 29 August 1514 and, as the fire broke out during his term of office, it could only have done so on the following 31 July – in 1515.

This was precisely as described by Adams and confirmed her view that the mention of Henry VIII in the generally accepted version was erroneous and highly misleading. It also supported her explanation of the discrepancy between the locally accepted date of a visit to the area by Henry VIII (August 1537) and other sources that put the King's visit in August the following year.

It seems that the evidence in support of Adams is overwhelming and, somewhat late in the day perhaps, the time has come to recognise that the generally accepted date of 31 July 1514 is wrong and that 31 July 1515 should now be adopted as the date of the Great Fire of Smallhythe.

Where the Fire Started

Over the years the river bank at Smallhythe had probably become cluttered with the paraphernalia of shipbuilding, the supplies and waste of specialist workmen such as blacksmiths and wood carvers, merchants' stores, warehousing and, of course, timber, timber, timber. In today's terms, Smallhythe was probably a health and safety nightmare, a disaster waiting to happen. On 31 July 1515 it did. Smallhythe was consumed by fire.

We don't know how or where the fire started. It may have been carelessness with a lighted flame, a lightning strike or a simple accident that caused Smallhythe to erupt in fire in the warmth of the last day of July. The summer heat, the thatched roofs of cottages and other buildings and the years of accumulated timber, shavings, pitch and tar in the shipbuilding area together would

have provided ideal conditions for the fire quickly to take hold.

Given the amount of shipbuilding activity at this time – Smallhythe was then at its peak as a major centre of shipbuilding and repair – there is a strong possibility that the fire started among the timbers, wood chippings and detritus lying on the bank of the river. Another possibility is that the fire started in one of the many thatched buildings in the village, where fire was an ever present danger. Perhaps one of the many craftsmen making fixtures and fittings for use in the ships, such as the blacksmith, was the source. Another possibility is that it could have been a spark from a domestic hearth that settled on something flammable like a wool rug or a piece of clothing thrown over the back of a chair.

From an original painting by Ron Batterbee

The Spread and Impact of the Fire

We believe that most of the houses in Smallhythe were timber-framed and clad with timber or other combustible materials. Many of the roofs would have been thatched. In this environment, it is possible to imagine a gust of wind picking up a piece of lighted material, lifting it into the air and then dropping it onto a tinder dry roof, setting it alight. The wind would then have picked up further pieces of lit material and dropped them onto other roofs. Soon, fires would have erupted everywhere.

The villagers, suddenly aware of the blaze, would have been unable to do much to combat it. All they would have had at their disposal to fight the blaze would have been sticks, brooms and buckets of water. Once the roofs were alight, they would have dropped lighted material around the outside and into the heart of the homes and other buildings and the fires would then have spread everywhere, consuming everything in their path. Nothing the inhabitants could have done would have stopped the flames from spreading through the entire village, from the shipyards and landing stages on the river to beyond the chapel to the north.

After rescuing what they could of their possessions, the villagers would have had to stand and watch as their homes, chapel, taverns, landing stages, trading houses, warehouses, businesses and their tools of trade were all consumed by fire. Smoke billowing into the air would have been visible for miles. The air would have been filled with the harrowing sound of crackling thatch and timber, exploding barrels of pitch and tar and, not least, the screams of anguish of those who could see their lives going up in flames right before their eyes.

Eventually the fire would have reached the outer limits of the village and died out. The scene would have been one of utter devastation. All that would have remained would have been charred timbers and an all-pervading smell of smoke and burning. Homes, shops, merchants' stores, shipyards all suffered the same fate, as did the

chapel, also built of wood. Everywhere would have been covered in black soot and ash. For days, if not weeks, the air would have been laden with the smell of smoke from the still smouldering embers.

Extent of the Fire

The physical extent of the fire cannot be determined precisely but there are two properties standing today in Smallhythe that may have been built before the Great Fire or may have pre-fire elements. Assuming that one or the other is correct and we plot them on a map of Smallhythe, we can deduce approximately the outer limits of the fire.

One of these buildings, a house, lies just to the north of Smallhythe church and the present day vineyard. We know for certain that the then chapel was lost in the fire. We can therefore reasonably speculate that the northern limit of the fire was somewhere between the church and the house.

The other building that might have pre-fire elements lies about 700 metres west of the road that bisects the village. Again, it is reasonable to assume that the fire did not reach this point. It is also a fair assumption that the shipbuilding area along the north bank of the River Rother and the port facilities were within the fire zone, the River Rother marking the southern extent of the fire.

Putting all of this together we can say that the extent of the fire may have been as indicated on the map opposite.

Smallhythe – From Ships to Sheep

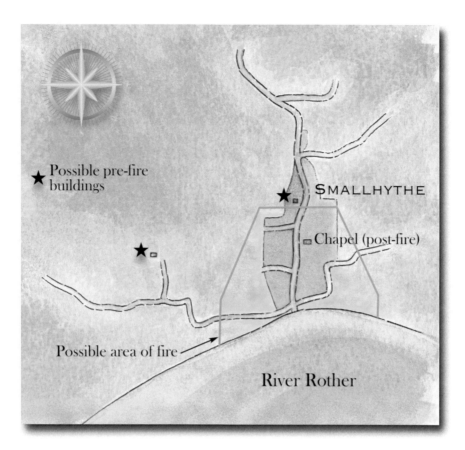

Rebuilding the Community

Despite the destruction, the inhabitants of Smallhythe were not prepared to give in to the conflagration. It helped that the community had grown rich on the back of shipbuilding and therefore had the necessary financial resources to allow them to rally round and resolve to rebuild everything that had been lost. Within a short period, construction work was underway. Houses, warehouses and other buildings were rebuilt and shipbuilding restarted on the river bank. Among the first of the buildings to rise from the ashes was a new chapel, built this time with brick and stone. The new chapel was probably started in 1516-17 and is still standing today. There is further information about aspects of the funding of the new chapel in Chapter 5.

The damage to the village was so extensive that repair work went on for almost a decade but by the mid-1520s it seems from church records that the immediate rebuilding phase had passed. The fire had doubtless been a great calamity, causing untold destruction and misery for the people of this small inland port and shipbuilding site, but at the same time, the inhabitants appear to have reacted with one mind and quickly re-established themselves and their reputation as one of the premier shipbuilding centres in England. Unfortunately, within 50 years the glory days for Smallhythe would be over. The river, having given so much to the hamlet, began to silt up and would eventually achieve what the Great Fire of Smallhythe did not – the end of shipbuilding at Smallhythe.

The east window, St John the Baptist Church

CHAPTER 5

Chapel and Church

Tony Buttler

The chapel at Smallhythe before the fire of 1515 formed a focal point for local residents who perceived and used it in a different way to their parish church of St Mildred's in Tenterden. Although difficult to imagine when making the five-minute drive on the modern road, for centuries the three-mile journey was regarded as difficult and sometimes dangerous and the people of Smallhythe were happy to pay for the upkeep of their own chapel and priest.

The chapel was dedicated to St John the Baptist (as is the present church) no doubt on account of his role as a baptiser in the River Jordan which made him an ideal guardian of Smallhythe's economic life, dependent as it was on the River Rother.

It is not known when and by whom the original wayside chapel was first founded or built but it is certain that a chapel stood on its present site at the end of the 14th century, although the present edifice dates from the early years of the reign of Henry VIII.

The Original Chapel

The earliest reference to the chapel is to be found in the records of the Corporation of New Romney in connection with shipbuilding where the accounts of that town show an entry in 1400-1 during the reign of Henry IV: '*Paid to the Chapel of Smallhythe at the launch of a barge named Eneswithe – 3s 4d*'. The chapel may at first have been but a small wooden building erected for the convenience of those who lived in a dreary water-logged district and at a distance from St Mildred's. It would, no doubt, have been licensed from time to time as a chapel of ease to St Mildred's and, standing near the waterside, was doubtless used frequently by seafaring men and strangers.

Smallhythe Pre-Reformation

Provision for religious services and devotion at Smallhythe was enhanced and even transformed in the early 16th century and residence there entailed heightened financial pressure upon families. This is reflected in the provisions of their wills which show their determination to retain their own chapel.

The competing demands of the parish required choices concerning the re-distribution of family resources at death, but this only appears to have been the case for residents of Smallhythe, whose particular piety was intensely localised and closely tied to distinctive environmental conditions and specialised economic development.

There are comparatively few references to the early chapel, those which are available being extracts from wills of the inhabitants in the form of bequests etc. between 31 May 1463 and 10 May 1503. About this time the status of the chapel was evidently regarded as being uncertain and an effort was made by one of the inhabitants named John Tyler to have it placed on a more sound basis by obtaining a permanent licence for the performance of divine service therein. In his will dated 1 June 1503 he instructs his executors to purchase, from the realisation of his lands, a perpetual licence from the Court of Rome to have a priest in the chapel. Probate of the will was granted on 18 March 1504 and there is no doubt that the bequest accomplished its object since the inhabitants of Smallhythe undertook to defray all expenses of their chapel and of the licensed chaplain. On 10 February 1506 Archbishop William Warham (below) formally licensed the chapel for divine service.

At this time there were disputes between the inhabitants of Smallhythe and the vicar of Tenterden over the duties of the chaplain and over money. The people of Smallhythe wanted their own chapel and chaplain – all of which they provided at their own expense – because of the *'excessive distance'* they had to travel to St Mildred's and also on account of *'the perils of the journey, the dangerous condition of the roads, the great floods and the sharp severity of the weather'*. Three years later on 3 May 1509 the archbishop issued a further order regulating the appointment of the chaplain and his position with regard to the vicar of Tenterden, defining and limiting the privileges of the people of the hamlet in respect of their chapel, and guarding the rights of the vicar and parishioners of St Mildred's against infringement. Under this ordinance the inhabitants of the hamlet were bound to support their chapel and chaplain at their own cost, and to find all things necessary for the celebration of divine service. Nevertheless, they paid their accustomed dues to St Mildred's which they attended on the great festivals and, with certain exceptions, for all the sacraments and for the burial of the dead. They also enjoyed the unusual privilege of appointing their own chaplain, subject to confirmation by the vicar of Tenterden. This privilege was shared by no other place in the county. The chapel was burnt down in the fire of 1515 and the present church (designated a chapel until 1865) was built to replace it.

Lollardy in Tenterden

From the 1420s, Tenterden was the place in Kent most associated with Lollardy which was a political and religious movement that existed up to the Reformation and was initially led by John Wycliffe. Lollards believed that the Catholic Church had been corrupted by temporal matters which distracted priests from other work and that effort should be placed on helping the needy and preaching, rather than working on expensive decorations. Lollards began the movement towards a translation of the Bible into English.

The Wycliffe heresy was embedded in Tenterden and the neighbouring parishes. The Wealden Lollards practised and passed on their beliefs through leading literate figures who transmitted and taught the new and controversial ideas through a loose network of heretical groups and households across Kent. Tenterden was a centre of dissent but, compared to the rest of the parish, piety at Smallhythe was austere and Lollardy does not appear to have been particularly strong.

Smallhythe Post-Reformation

At the time of the Reformation the chapel came very near to being suppressed under the Act of Parliament passed in 1547, the first year of the reign of Edward VI, which granted all colleges, chantries, free chapels, etc. to the King. Indeed, it seems as if it was suppressed or at any rate disused for a short time, but ultimately restored to the inhabitants. In due course the property was alienated to the Crown and there appear to have been various applicants to purchase it.

John Rowland, Page of the Robes to King Edward VI and Member of Parliament for the Winchelsea Constituency, bought it and he intended to have the chapel taken down, although, having been rebuilt after the fire, it had stood for little more than 30 years.

His proposal aroused opposition from the inhabitants, who were not at all disposed to submit tamely to the loss of their place of worship, maintaining that it did not come under the Act. So John Rowland found that he was not to enjoy undisturbed possession of his newly-acquired property.

To save their chapel from any further desecration, a lengthy and quaintly worded petition in 1549 was drawn up in the names of 12 of the principal residents, emphasising that the chapel had been built by themselves at their own cost, that they provided for the minister and that it had been wrongly conveyed to the Crown. It was pointed out that *'it would take an hour to get to St Mildred's and an hour to get back and the King's enemies would get to hear about it and would come and burn the King's ships when the inhabitants were away worshipping at St Mildred's nearly three miles distant'*. The petition duly reached its destination and had the desired effect as the resultant enquiry shows that John Rowland had to restore the property to the inhabitants.

So the chapel was saved and remains to this day. The enquiry indicates the character of the religious privileges enjoyed before the Reformation by the inhabitants of Smallhythe under the grant of Archbishop William Warham. It also shows the immediate effect of the Reformation in the spiritual destitution of the people, affording evidence of the decay of the haven and its ship-building industry. In spite of the restoration of the alienated endowments of the chaplaincy, there is no evidence of the presence of a minister for the next 20 years and even then it was only a Reader who was authorised to read, privately, the Holy Scripture to the sick and the aged and, publicly, certain portions of Morning and Evening Service in the Book of Common Prayer. Moreover, records of archidiaconal visitations towards the end of the century suggest that the people of Smallhythe did not consider the arrangement very satisfactory. Early in the 17th century the duty seems to have been performed by an assistant curate of Tenterden, Percival Brett, whose record was very unsatisfactory and who was dismissed for embezzlement.

The Book of Common Prayer is still being used for services in the 21st century.

The New Chapel

Following the fire on 31 July 1515, the inhabitants decided that they should continue to have their own place of worship and, accordingly, the present building was erected in 1516-20.

This is the building we have on the site today and the earliest known picture (above) is a water-colour dated 1809.

The people of Smallhythe appear to have promised to fund the chapel themselves, any outstanding pledges being dealt with in their wills. The first known case was the probate of a will made by John Donett dated 7 February 1516 from which it would appear that he promised a certain amount, paying a portion per year, but had not given the whole amount when he made his will. He therefore bequeathed a sum sufficient to pay the balance on his death. There were further bequests made within the next 20 years and some interesting items may be found among them such as:

- Robert Brigenden dated 19 November 1517 – *to the glazing of one window in the chapel and to the building of a house for the priest celebrating in the chapel to occupy and live in.*

- John Wayte dated 8 April 1526 – *to buy a chalice for use in the chapel and to the mending of the footway.*

- Robert Hovynden dated 28 April 1527 – *to the mending of the footway.*

- George Haryson dated 4 May 1527 – *to the light of St Barbara in the chapel* – which indicates that there was an altar, image or light dedicated to the saint.

The building (below) is in the shape of a simple rectangle and is substantially buttressed. It is unusual in its use of red brick for its construction and it is thought that the bricks may have been imported from the Low Countries in

exchange for timber from the Weald of Kent. The stepped east and west gables indicate a Dutch influence probably arising from the long-term trade links and immigration and, possibly, the employment of continental bricklayers. Whilst it is recorded that the porch was added in 1866, the brickwork and the picture on page 55 indicate that it was constructed earlier.

The oldest features in the church are the medieval oak screen (above left) and the wainscot panelling. The panelling is mentioned in the records of the local history society as the oldest oak panelling known to exist anywhere. The oak screen was carefully repaired in 1900 at which time extensive alterations were made to it, and the pews in the nave (above left and right), which are made of pitch pine, replaced oak family boxes.

The roof is a perfect example of a rectangular Tudor roof with two interesting repairs in evidence.

The roof over the chancel was repaired in 1747 by oak side purlins fixed at right angles to the rafters. The roof over the west end was repaired in 1982 by the addition of steel brackets and stainless steel straps on top of the beams. These are fixed to wall plates set in concrete spreader beams on top of the walls, almost invisible, and so preserving the antiquity of the building.

A statuette of St John the Baptist (above) was installed in the niche high up on the west gable in 1907.

The Windows

There are six windows and all are filled with stained glass which is unusual for a comparatively small parish church. The stained glass in five of the windows was made by Hemming & Co of London.

The west window (above) contains the only original Tudor tracery. It has five lights in late perpendicular style and crossed by a transom. In 1884 it was repaired and filled with stained glass in memory of John Curteis, a prominent Tenterden merchant. The lights depict episodes from the life of St John the Baptist.

Also in 1884, the window in the north wall of the chancel (bottom left) was filled with stained glass depicting the words spoken by Jesus to Mary Magdalene "noli me tangere" (touch me not); Jesus with two of his disciples at Emmaus; doubting Thomas and at the Sea of Tiberias.

In 1884/1885 the two south windows were restored at the expense of the Rev Arthur Wilkin who was one of the feoffees (trustees) of the church and in whose memory the reredos (carved in oak to match the old screen) was erected.

The lights in the window of the nave (above) depict the annunciation; the nativity; the flight into Egypt and Jesus with the doctors in the temple.

The lights in the window in the chancel (opposite top left) depict Jesus raising from the dead Jairus's daughter; the son of the widow of Nain; Lazarus and the three Marys at the tomb.

vestry in 1901/1902. The lights contain the inscription: "Why seek ye the living among the dead" and depict the three Marys at the tomb.

It was to the memory of the Rev Arthur Wilkin that stained glass (above) was installed in the window in the north wall of the nave above the

Originally the east window (above) was of four lights and plain, but it was altered in 1884 to three lights and filled with glass representing the Baptism, Crucifixion and Ascension of our Lord. This window was destroyed by a V1 Rocket in 1944 and replaced by the War Damage Commission in 1952 with the present window depicting Christ victorious, with a Paschal lamb and a medieval ship. It was made by A.W. Wilkinson.

The Church Furniture

The organ (below) was presented by the Rev Arthur Wilkin and installed by Mack of Great Yarmouth on 29 January 1886.

It was replaced with the present day font (below) which has been referred to as dating from the 15th century but it is in fact late Victorian and is made of oolitic limestone (granules of limestone bonded together with carbonate of lime). It is mounted on a mill stone from the grounds of Smallhythe Place and was installed in 1952.

The pulpit and lectern were gifts from St Mildred's in 1900.

In 1905 further gifts were made to the church with the erection of choir stalls and a screen of carved oak, which enclosed a vestry in the north-west corner. It was copied from one in a church in Somerset but executed locally.

The original font (top right) was very ornate and made of Italian alabaster and had been given in memory of the Rev Arthur Wilkin in 1905. This font was sold in 1952 to Swiss Cottage Roman Catholic Church in London for £35.

A list of the clergy of St John the Baptist can be found in Appendix 1 on page 75.

The War Memorial

The War Memorial is situated in the church-yard and was unveiled on 20 July 1920 by the Earl Beauchamp, Lord Warden of the Cinque Ports.

The memorial is a wayside cross of Gothic design in red Hollington stone and was designed by George Elgood of Tenterden.

The memorial records the deaths of six residents of Smallhythe who were killed in action during World War One, five of whom lost their lives on the Western Front in France and Flanders. The six were:-

18 June 1915
Lance Corporal William Walter Kesby (whose name is recorded on the memorial as his birth name of William Kesby Masters) of Spots Farm. He was in the Buffs (East Kent Regiment).

9 March 1917
Private Alfred James Ashdown of Ashenden Cottages. He was also in the Buffs (East Kent Regiment) and was part of the Mediterranean Expeditionary Force.

19 April 1917
Corporal Percy Alfred Austen of Cricket Field House. He was in the Queen's (Royal West Surrey Regiment) and was only 19 at the time of his death.

13 April 1918
Private Ernest Alfred Sharp of Ashenden. He was in the Middlesex Regiment and was 22 at the time of his death.

30 April 1918
Private Albert Edward Morris also of Ashenden. He was in the South Lancashire Regiment and was 41 at the time of his death.

4 November 1918
Private Frederick John Brunger also of Ashenden Cottages. He was in the Grenadier Guards and was only 19 at the time of his death.

Smallhythe Street, late 19th or early 20th century

CHAPTER 6

Then and Now

Susannah Mayor*

Today, Smallhythe is a collection of around four dozen properties, mostly homes dating from the 17th century or later. Many are located close to the section of the road from Tenterden that lies between the base of the escarpment to the north of Smallhythe and the bridge over the Reading Sewer (the local word for a drainage channel) to the south. It is likely that this stretch of road was once lined with houses, shops and other buildings.

The Reading Sewer follows the line of the north bank of the River Rother which flowed past this point in medieval times. Workshops and buildings serving the shipbuilding industry were located on the river bank on both sides of the road from Tenterden and were served by Strand Syde, a road which ran parallel with the river bank.

The escarpment is a dramatic, steep, wooded incline. There are a number of large houses and farms on the escarpment, set back from the road and enjoying sweeping views across the landscape to the Isle of Oxney in the distance.

It is impossible to be certain to what extent Smallhythe was rebuilt after the fire of 1515 without undertaking an extensive archaeological survey. The surviving records held at the County Records office in Maidstone are scant and often non-specific when describing parcels of land and buildings.

However, we can gain some clues by looking at the surviving buildings which we know to have been built just after the fire. These are Smallhythe Place and Priest's House, both high status buildings, and the Church of St John the Baptist. They suggest that the community held together and there was an appetite to rebuild domestic and non-domestic buildings. In these circumstances we can deduce that the working men of the village also rebuilt their homes, not least to enable them to remain in Smallhythe and to enjoy the economic benefits brought about by employment in the port, the restarted shipbuilding industry and its supporting and ancillary trades and in other commercial enterprises.

Smallhythe Place

Smallhythe Place, once the home of the famed Victorian actress, Dame Ellen Terry, attracts a steady stream of visitors and is now in the hands of the National Trust. It is a substantial building standing on what was the bank of the river.

The timbers between the main building frames along the front of the house and in the Entrance

*With thanks to Dr Judith Shaw of Smallhythe for her notes on construction of timber-frame buildings and permission to include her article on 'Care in the Commmunity'.

Smallhythe Place from the front today, showing the close-studding and overhanging upper storey

Hall are close together and known as close-studding. This was a costly form of construction, indicating that the original owner was a person of substance. It is of continuous-jetty design, with the upper storey overhanging the lower. Again, this is an expensive form of construction and a sign of wealth. Many of its original features remain, though over the years there have been some internal changes and the house has been reduced in size. At the back of the house, there is evidence of two wings extending eastwards, forming an open courtyard. At some point, both of the wings were reduced in size and the remnants covered with cat-slide roofs.

The room at the southern end, closest to the river, is the grandest room of the house. A diagonal beam, called a dragon beam, carries the jetty from the front of the house around the corner and along the south side of the house. There have

been a number of changes over time and some of the doors and windows have been blocked but it is clear that the window at the south end, unlike those in other parts of the house, was designed to be glazed, a new and very expensive innovation at the time it was built.

Glazed windows and chimney stacks go together because without a chimney stack the smoke from the fire would fill the room. The brick stack in this high-class end room created a comfortable and impressive space.

Unusually for this area of Kent, there is a cellar under the southern room. It appears to be contemporary with the original building and not dug out later. The walls of the cellar are made of a combination of materials such as brick and large lumps of iron stone and very large, water-rounded boulders, possibly once used as ballast in ships. The fact that the ground at this end slopes down to the river may have meant that it was necessary to create a sturdy foundation wall to support the house.

There were two doors next to each other at the front of the house, one led through the hall to the large room with its eleborate wall paintings and the other into the domestic and larger part of the house. The original purpose of the building is unknown. It has long been referred to as the Harbour Master's house but recent research has cast doubt on that; there is no record of a Harbour Master or Portreeve ever being resident in Smallhythe. Perhaps it was a shipbuilder's house with this large room overlooking the riverbank serving as his office. It could also have been an inn or a court house but this must remain a matter of speculation for there is no known documentary evidence of its original purpose. Whatever its original use, it became a farmhouse in the 17th century with a farmyard behind it.

The house and associated land was bought by Ellen Terry at auction in 1899, for £1,700. At that time it was called Hope House having previously belonged to the Hope family who owned much of the land in Smallhythe. Terry referred to it simply as The Farm and after her death it was renamed Smallhythe Place by her daughter, Edith Craig.

Behind the house is a barn which is believed to have been constructed in the second half of the 17th century, probably when the house became associated with farming. It is now the Barn Theatre. However, there is some evidence that the lower part of the building may date from the 15th century or even earlier. Although the structure of the roof belongs to the 17th century, several of the roof timbers are scorched and even charred, which could suggest that they were salvaged from the fire of 1515 or, equally plausible, that they were damaged by fire after the barn was built.

The barn is timber-framed, with weatherboarding to the lower parts of the external walls and daub infill above. It is a four-bay structure, designed to fulfil a multi-purpose function, incorporating cattle housing as well as crop storage and processing. In the mid-19th century several changes were made to the building to increase the crop storage area and various lean-tos were added to the outside. It has been altered further during its time as a theatre but care has been taken to preserve the fabric.

The Barn Theatre

In 1929, the barn at Smallhythe Place was converted into a charming little theatre. The theatre was the brainchild of Edith Craig, the daughter of Ellen Terry who lived there until 1928. Edith had wanted to turn the barn into a theatre during her mother's lifetime but Ellen demurred – she wanted to preserve Smallhythe Place as a refuge from acting. After Ellen Terry's death, Edith decided to go ahead with her plan, with a view to holding a memorial matinee on the first anniversary of Ellen's death. Edith established the Ellen Terry Fund and Memorial Matinees in 1929 and arranged a benefit at the Palace Theatre in London which raised enough money to get the barn ready even though there were holes in the roof and gaps in the timbered walls. She also refurbished a 19th century shelter shed attached to the barn for use as dressing rooms.

Small Hythe Place. Ellen Terry's Home 1902-1928. "The Barn Theatre" Small Hythe

The conversion of the barn to a theatre was achieved without damage to the earlier structure. The stage was sited at the west end of the building, partly within the old crop storage area, with the original seating, which comprised rough benches on a beaten earth floor, to the east.

In 1929, a year after Ellen Terry's death, Edith opened the house to the public and the theatre to invited audiences. The first performance on Sunday 21 July that year was a mixed bill of songs, theatrical sketches and piano recitals by local amateurs and visiting performers, including

Harcourt Williams, who became director of the Old Vic in London that same year, and his wife, the actress Jean Sterling MacKinlay. The performance, the first Ellen Terry Memorial Matinee, was conceived, arranged and directed by Edith and set the pattern for subsequent Ellen Terry memorial productions each July which usually included a substantial extract from a Shakespeare play.

Ellen Terry (left) and daughter Edith Craig in costume

The rough benches were soon replaced by 100 chairs (with rush seats) which Edith bought for 5 shillings (25p) each. She then 'sold' them to patrons for £1 each, the 15 shillings (75p) profit on each going towards financing the theatre. The "purchasers" had their name engraved in pokerwork on the chair back.

In 1932 Edith established the Barn Theatre Society, running it on a subscription basis in much the same way as the Society runs today. She put on five or six plays each summer. There was nothing like it in this part of Kent and up until the Second World War the Barn Theatre was a dramatic centre for the area. Edith died in March 1947 but the theatre lived on run by a committee chaired by John Gielgud and assisted by Dame Sybill Thorndike, Harcourt Williams and

Sir Lewis Casson. It now features a season-long programme of productions by visiting artistes to supplement those of the Barn Theatre Society.

In 1997 (150 years after Ellen Terry's birth) a 'theatrical angels' appeal was launched to raise further funds. Angels who donated £100

The Barn Theatre, with the original wooden chairs

were given a certificate; Guardian Angels who donated £1,000 had their names put on the back of the original rush-seated chairs. There were 22 Guardian Angels, including Sir Paul McCartney and his first wife Linda who lived near Rye, and the theatre owner and impresario Sir Cameron Macintosh.

In 2004 the floor of the seating area was partly dug out to allow for new tiered seating and other changes were made to comply with health and safety regulations, including a new sprinkler system, and a public licence was granted transforming it from a private theatre society into a public venue. In 2007, the front part of the stage was rebuilt but, in a few years, it was clear that the whole stage needed to be rebuilt. This was done over the winter of 2013/14. At the same time, The Green Room and the dressing room were insulated and refurbished. Despite these changes, the theatre still has the rustic look and feel of Edith Craig's creation and looks set fair to deliver a full programme of productions in a unique environment for many years to come.

Maurice Dalton

Priest's House

The timber-framed house to the south of the church was also renamed by Edith Craig in the first half of the 20th century. Previously it was known as The Cottage. Possibly she believed it had had a connection with the church but in fact the Cleric's house or Chapel house had been on the north side of the church and burnt down in February 1910.

that Robert Brygandyne, a noted Smallhythe ship-builder, may have lived there before moving to Portsmouth as Henry VIII's Clerk of the King's Ships, where he oversaw the construction of the *Mary Rose*. Like Smallhythe Place, Priest's House is a high-class building which displays wealth and incorporates design and materials that were innovative for that time.

Priest's House is a continuous jetty house but, unlike Smallhythe Place, the massive brick stack

From left: the former Cleric's house that burned down, the Church and what is now called Priest's House

Priest's House had been divided into two cottages in the early 1800s and only became one house again when Ellen Terry bought it for her daughter in the early 1900s.

This was probably the house of a merchant or clothier or of someone connected in some way with the industry or trade of the port. It is possible

was part of the original design and not a later addition. Thus the house had glazed and heated rooms from its very beginning.

The photograph above clearly shows the close-studding signifying to all the high status of the owner. The south wall is now weather-boarded but a survey by Archaeology South East, University

College London, in 2005 showed that the actual wall is very much plainer and not close-studded, suggesting there may have been a building immediately next to Priest's House masking it from those that the north wall sought to impress.

These two houses and the church are all that remain of the buildings of the early 16th century but together they tell of the continuing prosperity of the community at that time. We know from existing records that in the 17th century there were still at least two public houses in the village, The White Horse and The Swan. The former was located near the toll gate and is mentioned in various records from 1632 to 1706. The absence of any further mention in local records tends to indicate that it closed about this time. The Swan receives only two passing mentions in local records, both on 1 October 1662, and nothing more appears to be known about it.

There were also shops serving the community including, in the late 16th century, Henry Badcock's mercer's where he was described as living in a *'large timber-framed house and in considerable comfort'*. We know a great deal about the layout and contents of Henry Badcock's house and shop since many of his possessions are itemised in his will. On the ground floor were the hall, shop, parlour, buttery and kitchen; upstairs were a large and lofty bedchamber over the hall, another bedroom over the shop and rooms above the kitchen as well as two garrets or attic rooms. The shop stocked a variety of goods including Holland cloth, saffron, prunes, sugar, ginger, aquavite, silk, white pepper, quicksilver and gunpowder. There is nothing in his will however to determine where this building stood and it is not possible to identify it as an existing house, but it was clearly servicing a substantial community. Badcock had another equally well-stocked shop downriver at Appledore. The Smallhythe shop is thought to have closed by the end of the 16th century, a sure sign that life in Smallhythe was changing substantially.

Indeed, the harbour at Rye was silting up and the River Rother was becoming sluggish. New designs and bigger ships meant that Smallhythe could no longer supply the vessels that were in demand. In 1635, the course of the Rother reverted to its original route south of the Isle of Oxney and the topography of the area changed.

What had been water became agricultural land and Smallhythe turned into a quiet agricultural community sustaining fewer people than the shipbuilding industry had done. Consequently, the population declined. The final remnant of Smallhythe's connection with the sea fell away in 1924 when the last sailing barge to be seen there departed on its return journey downstream. In that same year, the settlement's small school closed and its building at the top of the escarpment became a private home.

The Ferry and Tollgate House

The ferry to the Isle of Oxney was an essential service for local people. However, no information has come to light about the vessels used and little is known about the ferry operators. In 1449, when representatives of Rye used the ferry on their journeys to Tenterden to negotiate the deal that led to Tenterden becoming a Cinque Port, the charge for a return ferry journey for the entire party was 4d (about $1\frac{1}{2}$ p). Other snippets of information reveal that in 1468, John Davies, who then owned the ferry, left it and other

Tollgate House

waterside property to his son Richard. Nearly two centuries later, in 1625, the Ferry House was occupied and probably owned by Richard Chittenden, for when his daughter Mary Chittenden was baptised, their address was given as Ferry House. A quarter century later, in 1650, John Carpenter, a barber-surgeon of Tenterden, bought the ferry and the Ferry House and a

Driving sheep through the toll gate

contemporary report notes that the river was still so wide "that no-one can cross there except in a boat or little ship". Eventually the river silted up, the land was drained and the ferry was replaced by a toll bridge controlled by gates at the northern end. When the change from ferry to bridge occurred is unknown but a map produced in 1688 shows a bridge was in place by then.

Little is known about the homes of the men who operated the ferry or extracted the toll on the bridge but at the beginning of the 20th century, the toll collector lived in a single-storey cottage immediately next to the toll gates. The cottage was also used as a shop where the wife of the toll keeper sold essential foodstuffs and other items. Photographs of the house indicate that it was small and unpretentious, on a par with an agricultural worker's house. The toll gates remained in use until November 1932 and were some of the last toll gates in England to be removed. Part of the gate was relocated to form a gateway into the grounds of Smallhythe Place, just to the north of the bridge. Tollgate House was destroyed by fire in 1956.

Yew Tree Cottage

Yew Tree Cottage stands opposite Smallhythe Place and in some respects is the most intriguing of the buildings at Smallhythe, giving us clues to an earlier, much larger building. It dates from 1770, after the commercial collapse of the settlement, so is not an old survival but its

Yew Tree Cottage, as seen today

Care in the Community

During the heyday of shipbuilding many more people lived in Smallhythe than live here now. But only occasionally, through the chance survival of a will or an inventory, do we get a glimpse of their lives and even hear something of their voices.

On 23 March 1564 the twice-widowed Agnes Young lay ill and close to death in a house somewhere in Smallhythe. She wanted to change her will and Dorothy, her daughter-in-law, had sent Agnes's maid, Joan Pollee, running to fetch two neighbours, Agnes Badcock and Elizabeth Brett, to act as witnesses. Agnes Young was bedridden and perhaps by this time she was becoming breathless. There was no time for writing. Agnes's son by her first marriage, Giles Pearce, later wrote down what had happened and recorded his mother's words exactly as they were reported to him by the women who were with her. His transcript survives in the record of wills for Tenterden and through it we can witness the very personal drama of that day.

The three women were standing close to Agnes's bed, the maid in the background, as they listened intently to her instructions:

"I pray you be good unto my maid and give her good counsel. For where I had made a will and given certain goods to diverse persons, since that time I have spent and consumed part of it and had it not been for this my maid I might lie here like a beast. Wherefore, I will that my maid, Joan Pollee, shall have all that I have."

Agnes's mind was clear but she was agitated and determined to have her wishes obeyed. Turning to her daughter-in-law, Dorothy, Agnes continued:

"Dorothy, I charge you upon my blessing that you take nothing from my maid, Joan Pollee."

"No Mother," Dorothy replied, "I warrant you my husband will take nothing from her."'

Almost satisfied, Agnes pressed on:

"No, Dorothy, you have had your part already and therefore, I charge you upon my blessing, take nothing from her."

All those who were around Agnes Young when she made her will belonged either to the farming or to the shipbuilding families of Smallhythe. After Agnes's death, her maid, Joan Pollee, the silent witness and beneficiary of the will, moved to live with Richard and Elizabeth Brett and it was in their farmhouse, two years later, that she died. What was Joan's inheritance? Not much; a little money, a few cooking pots and some clothes. In her own will Joan makes a careful division of her possessions between two teenage girls, perhaps her cousins, living in Appledore. Perhaps Joan herself had come as a young girl from Appledore to enter service in the larger, wealthier community at Smallhythe.

Dr Judith Shaw

construction tells us it was once the brick extension to an older building which has since been destroyed. The original part of the existing cottage has a large room downstairs with a high ceiling and another room above; tellingly it has a wide, enclosed staircase which is far grander than would be expected in a cottage of this size. The proportions of this extension suggest the building it was attached to must have been substantial; perhaps it was another building similar to Smallhythe Place, or perhaps it was the lost Swan Inn. The older part of the building must have been demolished by the early 1800s when the southern lean-to outshoot was built.

As agriculture became more important, new houses were built and many of the old, medieval houses were subdivided and occupied by farmworkers. However, in the 19th century with the coming of the motorcar, easy access from London and revived interest in vernacular architecture, houses like Smallhythe Place and Priest's House became fashionable country retreats. Trade, wealth and fashion were responsible for the construction of these houses and it was trade, wealth and fashion of a different age which rescued them from dereliction and saved them for us and the future.

Farming dominates the landscape in the 21st century, with the vineyard visible between the trees

During the 14th to 16th centuries, the River Rother flowed past this point and Smallhythe was a thriving inland port and one of the premier shipbuilding centres in England, supplying warships to several Tudor monarchs.

A ferry connected Smallhythe to the Isle of Oxney opposite.

On 31st July 1515 most of the village and shipbuilding facilities were consumed by fire. However the inhabitants quickly re-established the village and resumed the building of ships. Ironically, by the middle of the 16th century silting of the river heralded the demise of shipbuilding and the port. The ferry was eventually replaced by a toll bridge which continued to operate until 1922.

This plaque was installed in 2015 to mark the 500th Anniversary of the Great Fire of Smallhythe and to record the national importance of the medieval village and its inhabitants.

© Tenterden Town Council

Smallhythe 500
Commemoration Committee

Smallhythe bridge and plaque

CHAPTER 7

Whither Smallhythe?

Maurice Dalton

For the last two or three centuries, Smallhythe has been a haven not for ships but of peace and quiet, as if resting before embarking on a new adventure. The noise from the shipbuilding sites, the comings and goings of the port and the ferry have been replaced by the stillness of the countryside with just the bleat of a lamb, the song of a bird or, once a year, the roar of a combine harvester to break the silence. When shipbuilding was at its height, hundreds of people were employed in Smallhythe but today only a small handful of people actually work in the community, mostly in agriculture. So what sort of future is in store for Smallhythe?

Predicting the future is not something many of us can do with any great success. If we have a crystal ball, it is likely to be permanently cloudy. In many cases, predictions are little more than speculation or inspired guesses based on an assessment of what has happened in the past. Looking at the major events which have moulded Smallhythe it is clear that the circumstances at the time were likely to have been unique and, therefore, hardly a basis on which to try to predict the future of this small community.

For example, the construction of the Knelle Dam, with the unexpected side-effect of diverting the River Rother to flow around the north of the Isle of Oxney and thus sweeping by Smallhythe's doorstep on its way to the sea, was a one-off event hardly likely to happen again. Likewise, the deliberate breaching of the dam 300 years later, which led to another transformation of the landscape about Smallhythe, is not likely to be repeated. Nor is there likely to be a repetition of the fire that swept through the village in 1515. We can, with reasonable certainty, exclude this type of event from any speculation about Smallhythe's future.

There are, in Smallhythe, no outward signs of the medieval shipbuilding facilities, the port or the Great Fire. Just three buildings are certain to have survived from the immediate post-fire period. Few records exist to help us fully to understand life in this very special place. Consequently, there is no lingering fame, no museum devoted to this bygone age, no theme park capitalising on days of glory past. The only reminder of the past is a plaque on the road bridge at the southern extremity of the village reminding resident and visitor alike of just some of the stepping stones in the history of the community. The plaque was installed by Tenterden Town Council and Smallhythe500, and unveiled on 31 July 2015, exactly 500 years to the day after the Great Fire of Smallhythe.

The Smallhythe of the present has a contented feel about it. Visitors come to see Smallhythe

Place, the former home of the great Victorian actress, Ellen Terry, which has been in the care of the National Trust since 1939, to view the house and its fabulous collections, including many costumes worn by Ellen Terry in her long career, and to enjoy a wide range of productions in the charming Barn Theatre in the grounds of the house. Two hundred metres up the road, the church with its brick exterior, unusual gables and, within, carved wood panelling also beckons many visitors. A third, much newer attraction, established in 2001 just north of the church, is Chapel Down Vineyard, a producer of fine English wines as well as beer and cider. Between them the three quite different entities give some structure and a sense of permanance to the community of today.

What about the future? We know not whether an event might arise of such magnitude that it would have an impact on a par with the Knelle Dam or the Great Fire. If no such earth-shattering event occurs it might be tempting to suppose that Smallhythe will continue in its present way, enjoying the peace of the countryside, out of sight of the wider world. On the other hand, that might be underestimating the ability of Smallhythe to develop another niche activity or industry to the surprise of just about everyone. Perhaps the opening in 2014 of an art studio in the old church hall at the top of the escarpment above Smallhythe will be the catalyst for the creation of a new artists' enclave in the area. From this, a whole new genre might emerge, bringing fame and fortune back to Smallhythe.

Whatever the future for Smallhythe, whether the community waxes or wanes, thrives or declines, we should never forget the important role that the people of Smallhythe played in local commerce and in the defence of the realm, for century after century, particularly during the Middle Ages.

We hope that this book and the words on the plaque on Smallhythe bridge, reproduced below, will help to keep Smallhythe's incredible story alive.

During the 14th to 16th centuries, the River Rother flowed past this point and Smallhythe was a thriving inland port and one of the premier shipbuilding centres in England, supplying warships to several Tudor monarchs.

A ferry connected Smallhythe to the Isle of Oxney opposite.

On 31st July 1515 most of the village and shipbuilding facilities were consumed by fire. However the inhabitants quickly re-established the village and resumed the building of ships. Ironically, by the middle of the 16th century silting of the river heralded the demise of shipbuilding and the port. The ferry was eventually replaced by a toll bridge which continued to operate until 1932.

This plaque was installed in 2015 to mark the 500th Anniversary of the Great Fire of Smallhythe and to record the national importance of the medieval village and its inhabitants.

Tenterden Town Council

Smallhythe 500
Commemoration Committee

Commemorative plaque on bridge at Smallhythe

Smallhythe – From Ships to Sheep

Appendix 1

The Clergy of St John the Baptist, Smallhythe

c.1478	William Stanton	1705-1708	Humphrey Hammond – curate
c.1488-1491	Sir John (surname unknown)	1716-1736	Humphrey Hammond
c.1499	John Cogrell and William Cox	1737-1766	Richard Thoresby – became rector of St. Catherine Coleman, Fenchurch Street, London EC in about 1745
c.1503-1504	Sir William Edwardson		
c.1508	Thomas Hadokke		
c.1514	Robert Wise – became vicar of Rolvenden in 1522	1747-1749	George Adams – curate
		1750-1759	Richard Moore – curate
c.1516	Sir Thomas Ingreme	1760-1766	Daniel Chadsley – curate
c.1520-1523	Sir Richard Raye	1766-1812	Thomas Morphett – also vicar of Rolvenden and rector of Newenden
c.1521	Robert Idley		
c.1523	James Oldam	1812-1861	Thomas Curteis – became rector and vicar of Sevenoaks in 1831
c.1523 -1525	Sir Richard Londe		
c.1527-1533	Sir Thomas Crayke	1812	J. Beale – curate
c.1538	John Fuller	1825-1826	J. J. Monypenny – curate
c.1547	Peter Hall – also rector of Newenden	1834	Robert Twigg – curate
c.1553	Thomas Sawkyns	1847-1851	Thomas Milles – curate
c.1557	James Glathos	1861-1864	Alfred Henry Roxburgh – frequently absent owing to not obtaining his licence and other causes
c.1571-1573	Henry Stafford – became vicar of New Romney in 1586		
c.1576-1580	Robert Fowler – was pronounced contumacious (wilfully disobedient to authority) for failing to appear in Court	1865	John Alexander Drake
		1865-1867	Edmund Lilley
		1868-1899	Charles Thomas Pizey
		1899	Charles Edward Pizey
c.1589-1590	William Raynoldes – excommunicated on 5 April 1590	1900-1915	Walter Raven – Canadian clergyman and first vicar of Smallhythe
c.1592-1593	William Randall – excommunicated on 25 February 1593	1915-1921	Alan Bruce Ronald – became rector of Smeeth and rector of Biddenden in 1938
c.1599-1600	.... Rogers – read common prayer without authority		
c.1600-1608	Hugh Price	1921-1926	John Alfred Wood – last vicar of Smallhythe as a separate benefice and became vicar of Kennington
c.1611-1614	Thomas Greenfield – became curate of Lydd		
1617-1648	Isaac Ward – admonished for serving the cure without licence in 1618 – became rector of Snargate in 1648	1928-1932	Morrice Lionel Man – vicar of Tenterden
		1933-1947	Douglas William Winn Carmichael – vicar of Tenterden
1668-1671	Nathaniel Collington – became rector of Pluckley	1948-1959	Charles Stolto Wyndham Marcon – vicar of Tenterden
1671-1715	Stephen Haffenden – became resident in Egerton in 1671	1960-1965	Harold Willis – vicar of Tenterden
1671-1672	William Horner – curate without licence	1966-1974	John Francis Hough – vicar of Tenterden
1686-1687	Benjamin Horner – curate	1975-1982	Thomas Ewart Roberts – vicar of Tenterden
1688-1694	Thomas Fishenden – curate		
1695-1696	Robert Manby – curate	1982-1989	Patrick Alexander Evans – vicar of Tenterden
1696-1698	Benjamin Hollingworth – curate	1990-2010	David Geoffrey Trustram – vicar of Tenterden
1698-1704	James Mede – curate	2011	Lindsay Hammond – vicar of Tenterden

Bibliography

Archaeologia Cantiana published by Kent Archaelogical Society in the year shown:

Volume XIV (14) *The Early History of Tenterden* by Robert Furley, FSA (1882)

Volume XXX (30) *The Chapel of Saint John the Baptist,* Smallhythe by A H Taylor, (1914)

Volume XXXIII (32) *The Municipal Records of Tenterden, Part 1* by A H Taylor (1917)

Volume LXXVII (77) Paper 4, *Changes in the course of the Rother* by W V Rendel (1962)

Volume XCV (95) *Malaria: its influence on a north Kent Community* by Philip MacDougall (1979)

Volume CII (102) *Developments in the Lower Rother Valleys up to 1600* by Jill Eddison (1986)

Vol CXXIII (123) *An Archaeological Evaluation of the Medieval Shipyard Facilities at Small Hythe* by Peter S Bellamy and Gustav Milne (2003)

Archaeological and Historic Landscape Survey of Smallhythe Place, Kent by Mr Richard James, Dr. Gill Draper and Mr David Martin of Archaeology South-East, University College London (2005)

Care in the Community by Dr Judith Shaw. Previously published in the Magazine of the Parishes of St Mildred's, Tenterden, St Michaels and St John the Baptist, Smallhythe

Coronation: A History of Kingship and the British Monarchy by Sir Roy Strong. Published by HarperCollins (2005)

England's Medieval Navy 1066-1509 – ships, men and warfare by Susan Rose. Published by Seaforth Publishing, Barnsley (2013)

History of the Town and Port of Dover and of Dover Castle by the Rev John Lyon. Printed for the author by Ledger and Shaw (1813-14). Reproduction published by Bibliolife (2013)

Lollardy and Orthodox Religion in Pre-Reformation England by Dr Robert Lutton. A Royal Historical Society publication. Published by The Boydell Press, Woodbridge, Suffolk (2006)

Notes on Old Tenterden and the four Churches by J Ellis Mace JP, printed and published by W Thomson, High Street, Tenterden (1902)

Tenterden – A History and Celebration of the Town by Alec Laurence. Published by The Francis Frith Collection, Oakley Business Park, Wylye Road, Dinton, Wiltshire SP3 5EU (2004)

Tenterden – A Pictorial History of a Market Town in the Weald of Kent by R. S. Spelling. Published by Tenterden and District Local History Society (undated)

Tenterden – the First Thousand Years by Hugh Roberts. Published by Wilton 65, York (1995)

Tenterden's Houses: A Study of the Domestic Buildings of a Kent Parish in their Social and Domestic Environment by Judith Roberts. Thesis submitted to the University of Nottingham for the degree of Doctor of Philosophy (1990)

The Anthony Roll of Henry VIII's Navy Edited by C S Knighton and D M Loades. Published by Ashgate Publishing, Aldershot for the Navy Records Society (2000)

The Good Ship: Ships, shipbuilding and technology in England 1200-1520 by Ian Friel, Published by British Museum Press (1995)

The Shipwright's Trade by Sir Westcott Abell. Published by The University Press, Cambridge (1948)

The website of the Confederation of the Cinque Ports (www.cinqueports.org)

Acknowledgements

The contributors are immensely grateful to the following persons and organisations who have so willingly given their permission for them to draw on the works listed or who have otherwise assisted them.

Archaeology South-East (University College London) for permission to draw on their extremely comprehensive report "Archaeological and Historic Landscape Survey of Smallhythe Place, Kent April 2005", written by Mr Richard James, Dr. Gill Draper and Mr David Martin. This report has been a beacon of light to the contributors and has much influenced them in the preparation of this book.

Kent Archaeological Society for permission to quote or reproduce extracts from several volumes of its annual publication *Archaeologia Cantiana*.

Dr Jack Gillett of Tenterden for his invaluable advice and knowledge of local history and for permission to reproduce photographs and other items in his collection.

Ron Batterbee of Shadoxhurst for permission to use a part of his painting depicting the Great Fire of Smallhythe.

Tenterden and District Museum for supplying a photograph of the dress of a Baron of the Cinque Ports.

Tenterden Town Council for permission to reproduce the Council's photograph of their portrait of Rev J R Diggle by Daisy Radcliff Beresford.

www.roughwood.net for permission to use photographs of the Church of St John the Baptist.

Mary Adams of High Halden, a local historian, for reminding Smallhythe500 of her research into the year of the fire that destroyed Smallhythe early in the 16th century.

Smallhythe Place (National Trust) for allowing access to their photographic archive and for sharing local knowledge about Smallhythe.

John Weller of Tenterden for sharing his research on the Cinque Ports Barons.

The Confederation of the Cinque Ports for permission to reproduce images of a royal charter and the arms of the Cinque Ports.

Smallhythe500 for their financial support in the production of this book.

Laetitia Barnes of Afterhours Artwork who designed the book and drew some of the maps in it and to Anna Foster of YouByYou Books who willingly accepted the challenge of producing this book. It may sound trite and it has certainly been said many times before but it is a simple fact that we really could not have produced this book without them.

Picture Credits

Index

mall Hythe Smaled Smalede
mallede Smalhith Smallhith
mallyth Smalid Smalide Smallithe
malled Smallede Smalhed
mallhede Smallhith Smallhyth
mallhythe Smallhythe Smallid
mallide Smallit Smallyd Smallyde
Smalyd Smalyde Smalhed

mall Hythe Smaled Smalede
mallede Smalhith Smallhith
mallyth Smalid Smalide Smallithe
malled Smallede Smalhed
mallhede Smallhith Smallhyth
mallhythe Smallhythe Smallid
mallide Smallit Smallyd Smallyde
mallyd Smalyde Smalhed